TRANSFORM
YOUR BRAIN WITH
NEUROFEEDBACK

Transform Your Brain with Neurofeedback

Restore Your Focus, Reduce Anxious Thoughts,
and Revitalize Depressed Moods

CANDACE HOLMES, D.C.

For more information, email Dr. Holmes: drholmes@braincoreofduluth.com

ISBN: 979-8-89316-244-8 - paperback

ISBN: 979-8-89316-245-5 - ebook

ISBN: 979-8-89316-975-1 - hardcover

Get Your Free Gift!

 BRAINCORE NEUROFEEDBACK

Wait! ⏰

Don't forget your **Bedtime Bliss Blueprint.**

To get the best experience with this book, I've found readers who download and use my Bedtime Bliss Blueprint are able to implement faster and take the next steps needed to improve their mental health and wellness routines.

Want more?
Follow me on Instagram
@braincoreofduluth
for exclusive content.

You can get a copy by visiting:

www.braincoreofduluth.com/bedtimebliss

Dedication

To my effervescent, affectionate, and brilliant eldest daughter, Corinne,

Your resilience and outstanding work ethic have always been a source of inspiration to me. It was your journey of personal growth and transformation that led me to incorporate this life-changing therapy into my chiropractic practice. Witnessing the profound impact it had on your life sparked a change in my approach to mental health and wellness, making it the cornerstone of my practice today.

Corinne, you have shown me the power of perseverance and the importance of addressing the mind-body connection. Your story is a beacon of hope for others who are navigating their own personal paths towards wellness. May your light continue to shine brightly, illuminating the way for those seeking natural brain health options.

With unwavering love and admiration,
Your mom

Table of Contents

Foreword

In the pages that follow, you will embark on a journey through the meticulously detailed and profoundly personal world of neurofeedback therapy, as narrated by Dr. Candace Holmes. In "Transform Your Brain with Neurofeedback," Dr. Holmes merges her intimate experiences as a mother with her professional acumen as a chiropractor and neurofeedback practitioner to illustrate a compelling case for this revolutionary approach to mental health.

I met Dr. Holmes a few years back, and our shared dedication to non-invasive, drug-free health solutions formed an immediate bond. As someone who has dedicated over three decades to understanding and treating chronically ill patients, which hinders so many, I recognized in Dr. Holmes a kindred spirit. Her story resonates deeply with my own experiences, and her book is a testament to the power of personal transformation.

The book begins with a compelling narrative about Dr. Holmes' personal journey with her daughter's health challenges and developmental delays. She shares her experiences as a parent navigating various therapies and interventions, leading her to discover neurofeedback as a transformative solution not just for her daughter but for her patients as well.

She explains how neurofeedback is a sophisticated, non-invasive, drug-free therapy capable of addressing a wide array of neurological and mental health conditions. The book offers a detailed look into the history and development of neurofeedback, backed by personal testimonies, and professional insights. Dr. Holmes explains the scientific basis of neurofeedback, its potential benefits, and its application in addressing conditions such as ADHD, anxiety, depression, and more.

Dr. Holmes' transition from a concerned parent navigating the complex landscape of developmental challenges to a pioneer in neurofeedback therapy is nothing short of inspiring. It is a narrative that not only tugs at the heartstrings but also engages the intellect with its rich professional insights. Her approach goes beyond the traditional boundaries of health care, advocating for a paradigm shift towards more holistic, patient-centered treatments—echoing the very principles I've observed in my 35 years of practice and teachings as a chiropractor and integrative health practitioner specializing in thyroid and autoimmune disease.

This book does more than just inform; it invites us to reimagine our relationship with mental health and the human brain's remarkable ability to heal itself. As you delve into Dr. Holmes' world, prepare to be enlightened by her personal anecdotes, empowered by her knowledge and personal experience, and inspired by the promise of neurofeedback therapy—a modality that stands as a beacon of hope for countless individuals seeking to reclaim their mental wellness.

Dr. Philip Agrios

Self-Sabotage Specialist and Business Consultant

Best-Selling Author of "Life's One Law: Nature's 6-Step Blueprint for Repeatable Success"

www.TranscendNOW.biz

Introduction

Have you ever felt helpless watching a loved one struggle with mental health challenges, wishing there was a solution that didn't involve medication?

Locating a drug-free, effective, and almost permanent solution for mental health challenges in a world that was used to relying on medications was rather difficult. After seeking help from a child psychologist for my daughter who suggested that I place her on medications after completing multiple therapy sessions with her, I decided to press on. As a chiropractor, I was adamant about keeping her body free of all medications. That's when a chance article I read in a chiropractic magazine presented a drug-free solution called neurofeedback therapy. It has been in existence for over fifty years and is a viable option for those people as young as five years of age and older. It is non-invasive, has no side effects, has results that can last up to thirty years or more (some sources state up to fifty years), and drastically changed the trajectory of my daughter's life.

Upon completing this book, you'll gain a thorough grasp of neurofeedback therapy: what it entails, its functions, and how it aids our brains in self-regulation, fostering optimal performance. Within these pages, you'll encounter a collection of case studies—what I fondly refer to as case stories—from individuals in my practice. These narratives will captivate and inspire you as you witness the profound transformations my patients have undergone. Witnessing the remarkable transformations undergone by my patients serves as a driving force behind my decision to share their experiences with you. Their stories continually fuel my passion for spreading awareness about the remarkable benefits of neurofeedback therapy. By the end, you'll find yourself wishing you'd discovered it earlier, eager for your loved ones, regardless of age, to experience its benefits too.

Time is of the essence! Learning about neurofeedback therapy when my daughter was thirteen was a game-changer for her, me, and our household. Reflecting on those thirteen years before, it felt like an eternity of hardship. Had we known about this therapy when she was diagnosed at seven, our journey would have been radically different. I'm driven by the desire to spare you the anguish of enduring the challenges of mental health without this vital resource. My vision is for you and your loved ones to thrive, not just survive.

Go ahead, flip the page. Dive in RIGHT AWAY! The clock is ticking...

CHAPTER 1

The Road Less Medicated: Seeking Drug-Free Options

"If you can't fly then run, if you can't run then walk, if you can't walk then crawl, but whatever you do, you have to keep moving forward."
Rev. Dr. Martin Luther King, Jr.

I didn't know why my daughter wasn't thriving. She was born just two days short of full term, weighing a petite 4 pounds, 10.8 ounces. Although she was small, she was in perfect health. No NICU required. But as time went on, I noticed that she wasn't crawling. I put her in pediatric physical therapy, and then speech therapy when she started having trouble talking. As she grew up, I realized that she was a bit behind her peers in terms of developmental milestones.

She faced challenges as early as pre-Kindergarten. Enrolled in a Montessori school, she would stand on tables, trip her classmates, and more. I was concerned that she was constantly getting into trouble, and I wondered if Montessori was the right structure for her. Begrudgingly, I enrolled her in public school.

After a semester in kindergarten, her teacher suggested that I hold her back a year because she couldn't remember her sight words. I was devastated. All I thought was that if I had never enrolled her in public school, she would have advanced to first grade. But I was told that since she was already in the system, I had no choice.

I lamented about how I was to blame, since I had delivered her early due to extreme stress while working as an associate chiropractor. I discussed the situation with my ex-husband, who was supportive and reassured me that I was not guilty of doing anything wrong. He said that whatever I decided, he would be there for me. He suggested that maybe she would eventually grow out of whatever was going on. (Isn't that what we all hope?)

After much thought and prayer, I decided to retain her in kindergarten. She would now forever be the oldest person in her class. I decided to do this while she was in kindergarten since most educators, family members, and friends suggested to me that if I was going to retain her, then it was best to do it between kindergarten and the first grade. That way, she wouldn't really know any difference. It was one of the hardest decisions I had to make.

As she grew, she continued to struggle academically. Her younger sister was head and shoulders above her in terms of communication and social skills. I spoke with one of my first cousins about what was going on, and she suggested that I have my daughter see a child psychologist. The doctor my cousin recommended belonged to the same sorority as we did. I had met her years ago, before I was married and had children. I made the appointment, and my daughter was evaluated. She was eventually diagnosed with ADHD, or attention deficit hyperactivity disorder.

I was floored. Honestly, I was in denial. I thought the diagnosis was a catch-all, and very non-specific. I thought this was the diagnosis given when the doctor didn't know what else to do or to diagnose. I didn't know what my next steps should be to help her.

Over the years, I have become aware of the many avenues one can take to assist with a mental health difference or challenge. Here is a short list of approaches, a few of my patients have tried or have shared with me:

- Cognitive Behavioral Therapy (CBT)

- Prayer, Meditation, and Mindfulness

- Occupational Therapy (OT)

- Medications

- Nutritional Changes

- Speech Therapy

- Chiropractic

- Psychiatry

- Psychology

- Play Therapy

- Vision Therapy

- Mental Imagery

- Ketamine Therapy

- Eye Movement Desensitization and Reprocessing (EMDR)

- Melatonin

- Applied Behavioral Analysis (ABA)

- Counseling/Therapy

- Hyperbaric Chamber

- Tapping

- Cannabidiol (CBD)

- Dialectical Behavior Therapy (DBT)

- ADHD/Executive Function Coaching

- Naturopathy

- Acupuncture

- Music Therapy

Not such a short list, right? What I am told most often by those interested in neurofeedback therapy, is that they learned about it after reading The Body Keeps The Score by Bessel van der Kolk, M.D. For that, I am grateful. It also makes me realize how much I didn't know what was available or what was possible to help my daughter. What I knew for sure is I wasn't interested in ANY method that included medications. My daughter has such a bright light at the essence of her core and it has been there from the second she was born. Dimming that light by any stretch of the imagination was unacceptable for me. As a chiropractor, introducing medication into her body was against the core of my being.

As I searched for solutions for my daughter's challenges, I explored a multitude of methods, from the conventional to the unconventional. Thankfully, it was my commitment to a drug-free approach that led me to a game-changing article in a chiropractic magazine.

In the next chapter, we'll dive into the history of Neurofeedback Therapy. I will reveal an exciting path that could be the answer you have been looking for.

Testimonial by Lisa Priestly

Dr. Holmes fully assessed my needs, created a treatment program and provided the healthcare I needed. She is insightful and thorough. I recommend her fully.

CHAPTER 2

Neurofeedback: A History of Innovation and Hope

"If you continue to believe as you have always believed, you will continue to act as you have always acted, you will continue to get what you have always gotten. If you want different results in your life or your work, all you have to do is change your mind."

Anonymous

I used to think that being diagnosed with a neurological health challenge was a life sentence and that those with them were incapable of improving or changing. Now, I know this to be untrue.

Neurofeedback therapy is a sophisticated form of biofeedback that has the potential to help people with a wide range of neurological and mental health conditions. It is a non-invasive, drug-free therapy that uses real-time feedback to help people train their brains to function more optimally.

The history of neurofeedback therapy dates back to the 1960s, when researchers began to explore the possibility of using EEG (electroencephalogram) feedback to train people to control their brain waves. One of the early pioneers in this field was Dr. Joe Kamiya, who developed a method for teaching people to increase their alpha wave production. Alpha waves are associated with relaxation and focus, and Kamiya's research showed that people who could learn to increase their alpha wave production, could also reduce their anxiety, and improve their performance on cognitive tasks.

Another early pioneer in the field of neurofeedback was Dr. Barry Sterman. Sterman's research focused on the sensorimotor rhythm (SMR), a type of brain wave that is associated with motor control and attention. Sterman found that he could train cats to increase their SMR production, and that doing so made them more resistant to seizures. Sterman's research also led to the development of neurofeedback protocols for treating epilepsy, ADHD, and other neurological disorders.

In the years since the early work of Kamiya and Sterman, neurofeedback therapy has continued to evolve and develop. New research is constantly emerging, and new neurofeedback protocols are being developed to treat a wide range of conditions. Today, neurofeedback therapy is used by clinicians around the world to help people with a variety of neurological and mental health challenges, including:

- Epilepsy
- ADHD
- Autism
- Anxiety
- Depression
- PTSD

- Traumatic brain injury
- Stroke
- Chronic pain
- Learning disabilities
- Sleep disorders

Neurofeedback therapy is still a relatively new field; however, it has the potential to revolutionize the way we manage neurological and mental health differences. It is a safe, effective, and non-invasive option that can help people improve their brain function and quality of life.

Operant Conditioning

Operant conditioning is a method of learning that teaches people to associate their behaviors with consequences. When a behavior is followed by a pleasant outcome, the person is more likely to repeat that behavior in the future. This is called *positive reinforcement*. When a behavior is followed by the removal of an unpleasant outcome, the person is also more likely to repeat that behavior in the future. This is called *negative reinforcement*.

How Operant Conditioning Relates to Neurofeedback

Neurofeedback therapy can use the principles of operant conditioning to train the brain to function more optimally. For example, a patient with attention deficit hyperactivity disorder (ADHD) might be trying to decrease their theta brainwave production. Theta brainwaves are associated with daydreaming and inattention. The neurofeedback system can provide positive reinforcement to the patient when their theta production decreases. This positive reinforcement will help the patient to learn how to maintain a lower level of theta production, which can lead to improved attention and focus.

How Neurofeedback Therapy Works

Neurofeedback therapy works by using real-time feedback to help people train their brains to function more optimally. During a neurofeedback session, the client has detachable sensors that are placed on their scalp using a paste. These sensors detect the client's brainwave activity, which is then fed back to them in real time. The client can see or hear this feedback, and they use it to learn how to change their brainwave patterns.

Neurofeedback Therapy: A New Paradigm for Care

Neurofeedback therapy is a new paradigm for care that is based on the principle of neuroplasticity. Neuroplasticity is the ability of the brain to change and adapt throughout life. Neurofeedback therapy works by harnessing the brain's neuroplasticity to train the brain to function more optimally.

Neurofeedback therapy is a *safe*, *effective*, and *non-invasive* therapy that can help people with a wide range of neurological and mental health challenges. It is a new and innovative modality that has the potential to revolutionize the way we manage these disorders.

Forever the innovator, Dr. Richard Soutar, expanded traditional protocol methods by using a light driven, two channel bilateral compensatory training, that is used widely together with a database approach to protocol implementation that takes into account a person's biological, psychological, and social background. Dr. Souter is the co-Founder of BrainCore Systems which is the system that is used in our office.

There are two schools of thought when it comes to the use of the qEEG. One school chooses not to use the qEEG as a baseline and cares for patients or clients according to their symptoms. The second school of thought uses the qEEG as the baseline for the care provided to their patients and clients. I prefer to have a *baseline assessment* which provides objective documentation that clearly demonstrates the improvements the patient is making or achieving.

QEEG: A Brain Mapping Breakthrough

QEEG, or quantitative electroencephalogram, is a non-invasive and painless assessment of brain function. It involves placing a cap with many sensors on the patient's head and using a gel to conduct brainwaves. The patient then closes their eyes for one half of the time and opens them for the other half. The brain mapping process takes anywhere from 45 to 60 minutes, depending on the patient's comfort level and how still they can hold their head. This isn't always the case for those entering my office, but I do my best to make the experience as comfortable and relaxing as possible.

Back when biofeedback and neurofeedback were first being researched, they were only available at prestigious universities such as UCLA, Harvard, Stanford, the University of Tennessee, and Ohio State University. Since then, technology has improved and the software has become more user-friendly, making neurofeedback more accessible to clinicians. That is why I am able to offer it in my practice.

Neurofeedback therapy can be performed either in the office or at home. At first, I only offered neurofeedback therapy in my office, and patients would typically come in for therapy, two to three times each week. This meant that it could take months to years for patients to see results. In 2020, I began offering home units for neurofeedback therapy. This has drastically changed my practice model. Now, my patients can perform neurofeedback therapy in the comfort of their own homes and on their own schedules, without having to coordinate with my schedule. This is especially helpful for patients in Metro Atlanta, where traffic can be a nightmare! Having the ability to do neurofeedback therapy at home gives my patients the opportunity to have more brain training sessions in a shorter amount of time, which can set them up for success sooner. And since I am able to monitor their sessions remotely after they have been completed, I can still provide support and make necessary adjustments without them having to come to my office.

Takeaways:

- Neurofeedback therapy is a sophisticated form of biofeedback that was discovered, researched, and introduced in the 1960s.

- It has been developed by a plethora of researchers and has gone from occupying entire rooms to being available as a home rental unit.

- Neurofeedback therapy was first found to be helpful for people with epilepsy, decreasing the frequency of their seizures by over 60%.

- The SMR, or Central motor rhythm, plays a central role in brain self-regulation and can be trained to improve brain function (Sterman, "A Symphony in the Brain," page 46).

- Neurofeedback therapy can be performed either in the office or in the comfort of your home, thanks to advances in technology and software.

Now that you know a little bit more about neurofeedback therapy, the question I get asked most often is, who is neurofeedback therapy for? I will delve into that question in the next chapter.

Testimonial by Dr. Myron Brown

Dr. Holmes is a priceless gem in the Neurofeedback Therapy field. Her compassionate approach and deep expertise create a healing environment. Dr. Holmes' dedication to her patients' individual needs and her genuine concern set her apart. If you are seeking a knowledgeable and caring doctor to address mental health challenges, I wholeheartedly recommend Dr. Holmes.

CHAPTER 3

Trauma, Stress, and Neurofeedback: Navigating the Factors Affecting Brain Health

*"Education is the most powerful weapon
which you can use to change the world."*
Nelson Mandela

Before learning more about neurofeedback therapy, I thought that it was only for a select few in the population . Now, I know that it's for almost everyone.

Remember when you were growing up and thought that your childhood was average? Then, as you had more life experiences, you realized that not all families were like yours? Spoiler alert: every family is dysfunctional. Some more than others.

I grew up in a traditional two-parent family household. My dad worked as a pharmaceutical sales representative, and my mom worked as a high school educator. I was born and reared in Detroit. When most people hear that I am from Detroit, they assume that I grew up in the suburbs. Wrong. I grew up in the city of Detroit. I realized that my upbringing was quite different from that of most Detroiters. On my block, my dad was the president of the Block Club. We knew all of our neighbors by name. On our block, we were a bit sheltered and protected because there was no street directly behind us. The street in front of our block was a major street, and on one side was a building. So, while there were two ways in and out of our neighborhood, the majority of traffic came from one major road.

Another unique aspect of our neighborhood in Detroit was that the majority of our neighbors were educators. We had principals and assistant principals as neighbors. We had one neighbor who was a reading specialist, my mother was the language arts educator, and other neighbors taught science and mathematics. All the subjects were covered. So, there was absolutely no reason for students to fail in school.

I went to a Catholic school from first through eighth grade. I wore a uniform more than anything. We weren't allowed to wear jeans in school until my seventh-grade year. We had one "dress up day" on the last Friday of every month. I had more trouble trying to figure out what to wear on a free dress day, since I had always been used to wearing uniforms. The worst thing to do was to repeat one month what I wore the month prior on a free dress day. Talk about sheltered!

I didn't know what divorce was until I was in the 7th grade. A friend of mine casually mentioned on a Friday that she was going to her father's house. "Your father's house?" I asked. "What do you mean?" She said that her parents were divorced. "Well, what does that mean?" I asked. "They don't live together anymore?" She said no, they didn't live together anymore, and they're no longer married. I was flabbergasted. I had no concept of what that meant.

Growing up in a sheltered environment, I was loved and supported, just like the other students at my school. We mostly had the same experiences, but I do remember one classmate who was one of seven or ten children. I noticed that her clothes weren't always so clean, and that was my first indication that perhaps she didn't have as much money and resources as most of the other students.

As I gained more life experience, I came to understand even more how everyone's childhood experience is different. From north to south, east to west, all are different, and all are valid.

One night, our doorbell rang. At our house, you can open the bathroom window and look down on whoever is on the front porch. That's exactly what I did at that time of night. I opened the window and recognized my neighbor from a few houses down. She was approximately 8 or 10 years old at the time. She came to the door and said, "I can't stand to see my dad hit my mom anymore." I was floored. Just remembering that brings tears to my eyes as I'm writing this. I had no idea that my neighbor friend was experiencing and witnessing domestic violence in her home. Eventually, her family got a divorce and moved away. It wasn't until later, when I started getting more interested in people and their experiences, that I thought about my neighbor and the other kids I grew up with. What kind of mental health challenges did they develop as a result of having that kind of violent exposure? Anxious thoughts? Depressed moods? Post-traumatic stress disorder?

I quickly recognized that I was blessed to have had the sheltered, loving, and protected childhood experiences that I did. You don't get to choose your parents, environment, experiences, or what you're exposed to when you're young.

After adding neurofeedback therapy to my chiropractic practice, I was exposed to a plethora of children and adults who had lived through and were survivors of traumatic events such as abandonment, physical abuse, sexual abuse, emotional abuse, verbal abuse, and more.

Typically, I had to ask the people who were telling me their stories to give me a moment because I truly felt for what they had survived. I was thankful that they felt comfortable enough with me to share those experiences, and I thanked them accordingly. One person told me that I was the first person she had ever shared her traumas with. She was in her mid-twenties. Imagine going through life and suppressing the negative experiences you've had. You either don't feel comfortable enough sharing them with anyone, or you try to share them with people in hopes that they'll believe you or at least be willing to listen. That's what frustrates me the most. We are here to help each other. Sometimes, we don't hear what we want to hear, but we hear what we need to hear, especially in the case of children. Typically, they do not make up stories regarding the negative and traumatic events they've been exposed to. Why would they? Those children become adults who are taught that their experiences and words don't matter. They do and they do, especially in mental health.

Neurofeedback isn't just for those who've experienced childhood traumas; it's also a fantastic choice for individuals looking to enhance their brain's performance. It's about being proactive as we age gracefully, rather than simply reacting to life's challenges. If you have a family member grappling with cognitive decline, or if you aim to keep your mind sharp as you get older, neurofeedback can be the answer. Getting older doesn't mean your brain has to turn to mush; neurofeedback therapy can help prevent that.

I personally incorporate neurofeedback into my life to reduce stress levels. There are specific protocols tailored to address various conditions and challenges.

I can vividly recall a moment after a neurofeedback session. It was around 11:00 in the morning when a friend called me. She asked if I had just woken up because I sounded incredibly relaxed. I happily informed her that I was indeed in a state of ultimate relaxation, thanks to the benefits of my recent neurofeedback therapy session.

What are some of the causes of mental health challenges? The first is any perceived threat. Remember fight or flight that you learned back in high school? When faced with a threat, perceived or real, the brain has to make a decision to either stand and fight, or run away.

Back in grade school, while outside during recess, I mentioned to a friend of mine that another female student was "fast." That young lady was in the fifth grade while I was in the fourth grade. At my school, kindergarten through fourth grade was on the first floor and fifth through eighth grade was on the second floor, so she was what I considered to be a quote-unquote "big kid."

Later that day, the young lady came up and asked me what it was that I said about her. What I didn't know was that one of her friends was around when I said that, and they had gone back to tell her. Well, after that, I hit her with my plastic Ms. Pac-Man lunch box and then I ran. I ran like the dickens. I ran like my life depended on it. I ran to the curb where my dad was supposed to be to pick me up. He was my getaway car.

But, guess what? He wasn't there. He was running late, as usual. My best friend ran after me and was laughing the entire time. My heart was racing, and I was scared more than ever before. I was constantly looking over my shoulder to see if she was going to come after me. She never did.

We played on the same basketball team and the same softball team after that, and she never mentioned it once.

Recently, in 2019, I had the opportunity to be a speaker on a panel at the National Chiropractic Convention in Florida. It is the largest gathering of chiropractors in the world. It was held in Orlando. I had already spoken and was set to drive back home to Atlanta. I stopped by Dunkin' Donuts to grab some breakfast. This is the only Dunkin' Donuts that I've ever known in the history of Dunkin' Donuts that did not have a drive-through, so I had to get out of my car.

I walked in and saw who appeared to be that same person. I thought, "What are the chances that that's her?" Then a person who was with her called her name and I said, "I thought it was you!" She turned around and said, "Candace?" We hugged, and she still didn't mention anything. I have come to think that perhaps I gave her a concussion and she didn't say anything because she didn't remember. I pray that is not the case, especially with the work that I am doing now. This story often comes to my mind when I think about those who have suffered concussions. Again, I pray that I didn't give her a concussion and that she just doesn't remember what happened. I still didn't mention it, though!

The second factor and threat to brain development is toxins, drugs, or vaccines. These typically contain elements that can harm the brain. Toxins can be found in water, paint, and even certain fish. For example, I was warned to avoid eating fish with high mercury levels, such as mackerel, swordfish, shark, and tilefish, during my pregnancies. Eating these fish could increase the risk of my newborn suffering from cognitive delays.

Vaccines and drugs also typically contain ingredients that can negatively impact brain development, even in small quantities. This is important because the brain is not fully developed until the age of 25. I remember when I was in college and tried to rent a car at 21. I was denied because I wasn't 25 yet. Years ago, some researchers for rental car companies must have come across this important detail and made a rule denying anyone under 25 years old the ability to rent a vehicle independently. If I knew then what I know now...

The third factor is emotional or physical trauma. This includes physical abuse, accidents (car, motorcycle, bicycle, slip and falls), loss of a loved one, witnessing violence, war, natural disasters, and sexual abuse. Emotional and physical traumas can result in conditions such as concussions, traumatic brain injuries, anxious thoughts, depressed moods, anger, sleeping issues, headaches, and memory loss.

The fourth factor is environmental or physical stressors. These include air pollution, water pollution, climate change, poverty, racism, crime, chemical stresses, and emotional stresses. Physical stressors include chronic pain, injuries, bacteria, and viruses.

The last factor is spinal subluxation, which is what chiropractors work to remove. A spinal subluxation occurs when a vertebra moves out of its proper position, impeding nerve signals from the brain to the rest of the body. A misaligned area prevents the body from receiving the correct messages from the brain. This is why adding neurofeedback therapy to my practice was a natural fit.

Great job! You have gotten through explanations of who neurofeedback therapy can help. Remember not all people are candidates for neurofeedback therapy. For instance, I do not accept patients who:

- Are not committed to the process.

- Have a spouse who is not supportive of the program.

- Are children whose parents are not in agreement.

One thing I wanted to make sure of is that we release the blame and guilt we have regarding how we were reared, how we were parented, and for those of us who are parents, we forgive ourselves and others for what we experienced that wasn't so great. We didn't know then what we know now. Let's accept that and do what we can now to make the next generation better than what we endured!

Now that you know who neurofeedback therapy is for, the next question that I am typically asked is "What does it do?"

Testimonial by Nita Patel

Dr. Candace Holmes uses cutting-edge technology for her neurofeedback therapies and brain mappings. By helping one person in the family, it impacts the entire family, and she is doing just that. I highly recommend her services. Thank you, Dr. Candace, for all that you're doing.

CHAPTER 4

The Power of Neuroplasticity: How to Keep Your Brain Sharp and Active for Life

"The first step towards getting somewhere,
is to decide you're not going to stay where you are."
J.P. Morgan

When I was younger, I used to think that I would ride my bike everywhere for the rest of my life. Freedom! Then, as I gained more life experiences and matured, I learned riding a bike isn't as fast as driving a car. Driving a car isn't as fast as riding a train. Riding in a train isn't as fast as flying in an airplane. What's best about learning how to ride a bike, besides increasing gross and fine motor skills, is once you've learned, you will always remember how to do it. Cue: neuroplasticity.

Remember that feeling you get when you learn something new like roller-skating, driving a car, playing a sport, or perhaps even learning how to skip a rock?

When I was around 10 years old, I remember my dad taking me to our local roller-skating rink. I first learned how to roller skate and thought that I was hot stuff. You couldn't tell me I wasn't the BEST at it. At that same roller-skating rink, I was introduced to my dad's friend and his daughter Ayana. Ayana was a speed skater. She participated in competitions at the roller-skating rink regularly. When I saw her wiz around those cones on each corner of the roller-skating rink with ease and precision, I was enthralled. My little roller-skating skills didn't compare in the least to her skills in roller skates. Nevertheless, I still got out on that roller-skating rink and enjoyed myself.

For years and years, my friends and I would meet up at the roller-skating rink every Friday night when I was in the seventh grade. Roller-skating was another sense of freedom for me. I was able to exercise, spend time with my friends, beat them in the Ms. PacMan, Donkey Kong, and Popeye arcade games, and form lasting memories all while grooving to the beats from the music of my youth. That was a fantastic time in my life that I will cherish forever.

The more people practice any kind of skill, the greater they will be at it. There is an expression that states that practice makes perfect. As I have lived more years on this Earth, I've heard that expression corrected to stating "perfect practice makes perfect" because if you are practicing incorrectly, then you will perform the skill incorrectly. Makes sense.

Years went by and I have gone roller-skating less and less. Recently, I contemplated throwing my 50th birthday party at a roller-skating rink. When I shared that vision with those in my age group, I had quite a few of them verbalized being concerned about falling. That did not ever even enter my mind. Apparently, they were more concerned about falling and perhaps breaking a bone than I was or even am today. I was more interested in reliving my childhood, getting in shape, and having a great time all at once.

As I think back to Ayana and her perfect speed roller-skating skills, I wonder if she is still skating at this time in her life. Is she still able to whiz around those corners and cones like she did back when we were younger? Would she be concerned about breaking a bone or falling while roller-skating?

Barring any unforeseen circumstances, she shouldn't be, thanks to what is called neuroplasticity.

Neuroplasticity is the way our brain adapts and reacts to new information. It is the foundation for neurofeedback therapy. When women are pregnant, they are encouraged to play classical music to the baby in their womb. Listening to classical music has been shown to increase a baby's cognition and overall ability to learn. New neural pathways are formed when we learn something new. Think of it as little highways in your brain. When we were younger, we may have just formed one-way roads. Then, we progressed to two-way roads with off-ramps. As we get older and learn how to speak, how to walk, and how to use our skills appropriately, more roads are formed in our brains. With each new skill learned, we construct more and more highways and expressways which result in more neural pathways being formed. Pretty soon, these superhighways allow us to go to more destinations in life. That's why we are encouraged while in school to read often. Reading exposes us to vocabulary we have not heard or seen before. When I was in school, we had to write down those new words that we didn't understand, look them up in the dictionary, and then use them in a sentence five times. This method encouraged us to use our new vocabulary words and expand our horizons as far as our minds were concerned.

Preventing Cognitive Decline

Our teachers were right! Reading a physical book with pages that flip is one of the best ways to prevent cognitive decline. Dancing is another great way to exercise your body and brain, especially when you learn new and complex dances. Try learning a new line dance, hustle, or shuffle. For even more brain benefits, improvise your own moves. Dancing is a fun and challenging activity that boosts brain function and power, increases your heart rate, and improves flexibility.

Another way to improve your brain and utilize the benefits of neuroplasticity is to learn new computer skills. New applications are coming out all the time. At the time of this writing, TikTok is quite popular. Learning how to record and post your own dance moves on social media is a great way to enhance neuroplasticity and form new neural superhighways. Even if you're not tech-savvy, there are simple things you can do, like learning how to record on your phone or send an email with attachments.

To further boost neuroplasticity, I challenge you to read for pleasure for 30 days. Choose a genre that interests you and inspires you to read daily. Keep a notebook handy and write down any unfamiliar vocabulary words. Then, look them up in a dictionary and use them five times in a sentence throughout the day. These simple steps will help you form new neural pathways. The more often you do this, the quicker your superhighways will form. So, get to reading! You've got this!

Now that you know what neurofeedback does, the next question most people ask is, "How long does it take to see results?"

Testimonial by Crystal Gonzalez

After seeing Dr. Holmes, I have so much more clarity with my issues. Dr. Holmes is patient and caring. She's very easy to work with. Very highly recommended.

CHAPTER 5

Learning Takes As Long As It Takes

"Choose to be optimistic. It feels better."
Dalai Lama

I used to think everyone learned information at the same rate and style. Now, I know that each person has their own unique pace and learning style. Our life experiences also play a major role in how we learn.

Growing up, my older brother would always wait until the last minute to complete his homework, typically right before he went to bed. This used to frustrate me to no end! I, on the other hand, couldn't wait to come home from school and finish my homework as soon as possible so that I could watch TV. My brother chose to come home and go outside to play after school each day. My mother would make me take off my uniform and relax for at least thirty minutes before diving into my homework. She understood the value of giving your brain a rest before putting it to work for long periods. No matter how hard I tried to emulate my brother's style, it didn't work for me. He could go to class without completing any homework and still earn an A on the test. I had to go to class, take copious notes, rewrite those notes in a more legible way, underline, circle, highlight, and then reread those same notes for the information to sink into my brain and remain there.

When all was said and done, the only way my brother and I were the same is that we both earned honors in history in grade school and high school. He was offered a full scholarship after high school. I was only offered a partial scholarship. I did my best to try and earn the same score as my brother on the ACT. I took that test three times and could not even get close to his score. My brother scored close to perfect on the ACT, and back then, the use of calculators was prohibited. Even though we were born and reared by the same parents, the ways in which our brains processed information were different. One way is no better than the other. What matters is how you use your strengths to your greatest advantages.

Learning takes as long as it takes... just like neurofeedback.

With neurofeedback therapy, the more often you perform it, the better, more efficient, and more optimized your brain becomes. With all the experiences, traumas, abuses, and unfortunate events that have played a part in the development of your brain, there's still time for your brain to make lasting changes. I call them transformations. Just like the way your brain is functioning now didn't happen overnight, getting the brain to change how it functions also doesn't happen overnight.

On average, a person with a straightforward case will see their symptoms decrease and improvements happen after approximately 15 to 20 completed training sessions. By a straightforward case, I mean one where there is an absence of underlying metabolic issues and deficiencies with the patient. When underlying metabolic conditions are present, they must first be addressed or in the process of being corrected before beginning a Neurofeedback Therapy program at my office. Because of this, I have wellness affiliates in the pediatric, adolescent, and adult populations who address these issues in an integrative manner using various natural techniques and methods. When moderate to severe metabolic conditions exist, it can take a neurofeedback therapy patient 2 to 3 times as long to experience results and notice a decrease in symptoms.

It should be noted that when one begins a neurofeedback therapy program in my office, the brain mapping performed using a qEEG is not a diagnostic tool. It is a functional assessment. When the report is generated, I am unable, by the results, to diagnose a mental health challenge or condition. Doing so is also outside of my scope of practice. Neurofeedback is a learning modality.

How long did it take Thomas Edison to perfect the light bulb? How many iterations did it take for Formula 49 to work? Trick question! How long will it take neurofeedback to work for you? It will take as long as it takes for your brain to understand what is happening and learn how to regulate itself. Changes in brain function can be seen within a few sessions, but most people notice significant improvements after 12-20 sessions. The number of sessions needed varies depending on the individual and their condition.

In the next chapter, I will share with you how I got started with BrainCore Neurofeedback Therapy.

Testimonial by Margarita Eberline

I had an amazing experience with my son. After trying to get help from regular doctors who did not have any answers for me, BrainCore made a difference in just a few weeks.

CHAPTER 6

From Natural Birth to Early Challenges: A Mother's Story

"Once you face your fear, nothing is ever as hard as you think."
Olivia Newton-John

I used to think that the best indicator of a newborn baby's health was its weight. Now I know there are many other factors that indicate optimal health and wellness for a newborn.

I gave birth to a bouncing baby girl at 36 weeks and 5 days. She weighed 4 pounds, 10.8 ounces. She was born at 9:44 p.m. Most of you would think a baby who weighed under 5 pounds would have to go to the neonatal intensive care unit (NICU). You would be wrong. My daughter was a healthy, 4-pound, 10.8-ounce baby girl. She was in perfect health...she was just petite!

I remember my parents were driving down from Michigan to Ohio to meet their very first grandchild. When I called my dad, he asked me how much she weighed. When I told him she weighed 4 pounds, 10.8 ounces, I could feel the stress and tension he was holding simply by the pauses and breaks in our conversation. "But it's okay, Daddy. She's in perfect health!", I told him. He let out a heavy sigh; however, I knew he was still very concerned about his new granddaughter's birth weight.

One of the things my husband at the time and I agreed upon was that she would receive no vaccinations, especially as a newborn. As a chiropractor, I was thoroughly educated regarding the ingredients and components used in vaccinations. Many are quite unfavorable, even carcinogenic. I told my husband his only job was to protect our daughter from getting injected. I halfway teased and threatened him to not make me get off the delivery room table to protect our child. That was his job...his ONLY job while I was in that bed. We did not allow her to have silver nitrate placed in her eyes, either, after she was born. I received so many compliments on how bright and clear her eyes were when she was an infant. I contributed that to her not having silver nitrate applied.

When I was pregnant with our first child, I was working as a chiropractor in Cincinnati, Ohio. I first came to work at that office as an associate. I was providing coverage for the owner doctor who was pregnant with her and her husband's second child. I had developed a wonderful relationship with her office manager. After a few months, her office manager let me know she had decided to move on to another profession. The owner's niece would be the new office manager. She literally just graduated with an undergraduate degree. She was now going to be my supervisor. Nepotism at its finest.

While the owner doctor was recovering during her maternity leave, the outgoing manager expressed one thing to me: make sure the new office manager/niece did not earn more money than I did. I was so surprised she would mention that to me. Surely, the owner would not do that to me.

Well, it was time for her to start working at the office. After she started working, I happened to be standing by the fax machine. At that time, everyone's pay stub came over the fax machine. As a result, I was able to clearly see with my own eyes in black and white that the new manager was making more money than I was. I was livid!

How could she do this? How could she do this to me? Here I was, a third-year chiropractor, and someone whose college degree ink was still wet was immediately making more than I was simply because she was someone's niece. I immediately thought of the former office manager and what she told me. She knew this was going to happen and wanted to prepare me. After finding that out, the rage I felt had me under a great deal of stress and pressure. Every time I saw the office manager and witnessed how clueless she was as to what was going on in the chiropractic office, I would get even more upset. And yet, she was still earning more than I was…for nothing.

I started spotting. Because of that, the owner doctor insisted I take a daily one-hour nap during our two-hour lunch break. Yet and still, my water broke at 36 weeks and 5 days. After all was said and done, I labored for only two and a half hours. I attributed that to being under regular chiropractic care and being trained on the Bradley Method® of natural childbirth.

The Bradley Method® teaches couples how to deliver babies naturally and vaginally without using medications. The husband is the wife's coach and advocate during the birthing process. One of the biggest differences I remember from performing the Bradley Method® was when the labor and delivery nurse started telling me how to breathe while I was in active labor.

The Bradley Method® taught me that my body innately knows how to breathe, no matter what situation is happening. Birthing a baby is no different. My body knew what to do. Thankfully, immediately after the nurse started telling me how to breathe, my husband stepped in, spoke up, and reminded me to breathe as I needed. I was both thankful and surprised that he spoke up when I didn't have the energy to do so myself.

The look on the labor and delivery nurse's face was priceless. It wasn't her fault, either. She was doing what she was trained to do. However, she was probably confused about why I was resisting her instructions.

The main reason why most women have oxygen masks given to them while in labor is because they are breathing in a way that is opposite from what is natural to the body. The Bradley Method® teaches women how to breathe deeply and rhythmically throughout labor. This helps to keep the mother and baby relaxed and oxygenated.

I highly recommend using the Bradley Method® if you are interested in having a natural childbirth. I do not receive any compensation for making this recommendation.

Early Motherhood

I was getting adjusted by my chiropractor at least twice each week throughout my pregnancy. I also maintained a regular prenatal yoga routine and ate a healthy diet. I did my best to relax and be calm.

When my daughter was born, she was unable to latch on to breastfeed. Her muscles were not strong enough to perform that function. I was instructed on how to massage her mouth and jaws in preparation for the day she would be able to latch on appropriately. It took ten weeks for her to learn how to latch on. I was dedicated to the process and there were lots of tears shed on my end. I'm grateful for a friend who kept encouraging me to stay the course. My daughter would eventually latch on. It seemed like FOREVER; yet she did it!

My daughter was in the lower percentile range as far as physical development was concerned. She also experienced developmental delays. It took her a while to crawl. She did not want to crawl at all.

Each time I put her on her stomach for tummy time, she would begin crying. Apparently, she thought that I was trying to put her to sleep, and she did not want to go to sleep.

I expressed my concerns to her pediatrician who told me that it was okay for her to start walking without crawling first. That was totally against what I was taught in chiropractic school. Babies are to crawl before they walk. When a baby crawls, they learn how to follow their hands each time they place them in front of themselves to crawl. It was an important part of the developmental process and I wanted to make sure she went through every step especially since she was petite at birth.

Her pediatrician prescribed physical therapy for her to learn how to crawl. I didn't even know there was such a thing at that time. She also had a challenge with her speaking abilities, so I was taking her to speech therapy appointments as well for months.

Moving to Atlanta

When I moved to Atlanta from Detroit after healing from a divorce, the girls were 3 and 5 years old. I was trying to figure out where to put them in school. I heard about Montessori school and wanted my daughters to have the opportunity to experience this type of learning environment so I enrolled them.

My youngest daughter was thriving; however, my oldest daughter was suffering. I was consistently getting calls from the school with complaints of her standing on tables and tripping her classmates. It seemed like the phone rang multiple times every day, hour upon hour. It was a very stressful time for both her and me.

It was clear to me that this educational learning model was not ideal for her. I thought she may have needed a more structured and traditional environment. It was then that I enrolled her in kindergarten at a public school. I enrolled my youngest in a pre-kindergarten program at a nearby daycare facility.

At the public school, the kindergarten teacher suggested that I retain my daughter. She had only been enrolled for one semester, but she was struggling to remember her sight words, which are essential for success in the first grade. I was hesitant to hold her back, but I spoke with my ex-husband, and he encouraged me to consider it. He also reassured me that it was not my fault. The mommy guilt was still strong, but I knew I had to do what was best for my daughter. We didn't want her to fall behind in her studies and feel discouraged.

I shared what was going on with my daughter with my first cousin. She suggested I take her to a child psychologist for an evaluation. I was already feeling guilty about moving from Detroit to Atlanta, and I worried that the move had been too stressful for my daughter. I was also still trying to adjust to being a newly divorced parent whose child no longer had access to her father as she did before. I blamed myself for a lot of it, but my ex-husband helped me to calm down and realize that I was not doing anything wrong.

Before I made the appointment with the child psychologist, I decided to retain the services of a naturopath who was also a licensed acupuncturist. I was determined to try to avoid medicating my daughter. She has always had a bright light within her, and I wanted to keep her spirit vibrant. I was not going to allow medications to dim her light.

The acupuncturist and naturopath evaluated my daughter and grounded her using magnets at particular locations in her ear. They then suggested that she take a homeopathic remedy, which are small pellets taken orally to level out hyperactive tendencies. The naturopath warned me that the dosage would change as she aged due to natural hormones and changes her body experienced as she grew.

At that point, I decided to schedule an appointment with a child psychologist. I made sure to choose a child psychologist over a psychiatrist simply to avoid the suggestion of medication. The initial appointment started off independently of my daughter. The psychologist wanted to know what was going on with me and with my daughter, which I appreciated. The process for her began and I was given paperwork to submit to her teachers, asking for their opinions regarding what they were witnessing and experiencing with her while at school. After all was said and done, the diagnosis she was given was that of attention deficit hyperactivity disorder (ADHD). She was only seven years old.

I was in denial. At that time, I thought an ADHD diagnosis was a catch-all when no one knew what else to call it. It was too broad for me. I didn't accept it. I started asking family members if anyone in our family had ever been diagnosed with ADHD. Nothing. Then, I asked my ex-husband's cousin if anyone in their family had ever been diagnosed with ADHD and she said, "Well…" I started shaking my head. There it was!

What I've come to know now is that ADHD is a normal variant. There is also a genetic component to it. Discovering that my ex-husband's side of the family had family members with that diagnosis put it all together for me. Now I'm not saying I was any closer to accepting it; however, I was a bit closer to trying to learn more about it.

I moved to Atlanta from Detroit in 2008. As many of you will recall, this was the time that our country was going through a recession. I was unable to find a position as a chiropractic associate before I moved. I was under the impression that companies thought that I wanted them to move me from Michigan to Georgia and that's why I wasn't getting any callbacks. Little did I know that no one was hiring. When I moved to Georgia, I changed the address on my resume and thought all would be well. That will fix it. It didn't.

I was struggling to feed my family. The only money that I had coming into the household was from child support. Thank God my ex-husband was paying child support! I was paying my parents rent when I lived with them after the divorce. I was so very thankful and appreciative that they took all the money I paid each month and kept it in an account for me. When I told them I was moving to Atlanta, they told me about the money they put away for me. That was the only reason the apartment complex in Georgia allowed me to move. I demonstrated that I had money in savings to last for a few months.

Between paying for Montessori School, childcare, rent, and overhead expenses, my savings were running out quickly. That was another reason I removed my daughters from Montessori School. I could no longer afford it. Times were so rough for me and the girls. It got so rough that my friends would bring food over for us to eat. A friend of mine who lived out of town had to tell me to go and apply for food stamps. I knew what food stamps were and I didn't think I needed them. She was the one who had a "come to Jesus moment" with me. She reiterated how I was in Georgia with no family and two mouths to feed in addition to my own. Food stamps were to help fill in the gaps if the bottom falls out. She had a point. I applied and was approved.

Another friend suggested I become a substitute teacher so that I could make some kind of money that didn't involve my working at a fast-food restaurant. I was a doctor for goodness sake! The thought of working in a fast-food restaurant sent chills up my spine. I liked her suggestion since at the very least, I would be among those who would appreciate the fact I earned my doctorate and would see that as an asset, opposed to a liability. I wouldn't run the risk of being labeled as "overqualified."

One day at church, I met a gentleman who noticed that I was new. He asked me what I did, and I told him that I was trying to become a substitute teacher. His eyes lit up. He told me that his son was an assistant principal at a local middle school and that he would be a great resource for me. I met with his son, who directed me through the process. At the time, substitute teachers made $87 per day. I later learned that we were only paid once a month, just like traditional teachers. But I was just happy to have the opportunity to earn some income and stop the bleeding in my financial life.

At the middle school where I worked most of the time, I met an educator who specialized in special education. I shared with her what was going on with my daughter. She was the first person to tell me that my daughter couldn't help the symptoms she was experiencing from ADHD, such as lacking focus and attention, being socially awkward, taking five hours on average to complete homework assignments every night, and struggling with comprehension.

She told me about two different types of educational plans: 504 plans and individualized education programs (IEPs). I told her that I didn't want my daughter to be labeled. She gave me the following analogy: she asked if my daughter had a physical challenge and was in a wheelchair, would I not build a ramp for her? I couldn't answer her without shaking my head. She was right. I would build her the best ramp that I could. How was this any different?

She said that she understood and suggested that I start by putting my daughter on a 504 plan. This would give her the opportunity to have accommodations set in place from her educators while in school, which would help her. I followed her advice and had my daughter placed on a 504 plan up until the sixth grade.

Then the Bottom Fell Out

Middle school was a brick wall for my daughter. The accommodations in her 504 plan were no longer effective since the amount of schoolwork had doubled overnight. Her stress and anxiety were palpable. I had to figure out how to help her quickly.

I realized that I needed to consider elevating her 504 plan to an individualized education program (IEP). I had been reluctant to do this, seeing it as a last resort. But the analogy from the special education educator came to mind: wouldn't I give her the best opportunity to be successful? She was struggling with challenges that were invisible to others.

I arranged a meeting with the head counselor at her charter school to develop an IEP. I brought documentation and the accommodations her child psychologist recommended. These included:

- Preferential seating in the classroom

- Partial completion of notes for fill-in-the-blank presentations

- Extended time to complete assignments, tests, and quizzes

- Taking tests and quizzes in a small group away from the rest of the class

- Breaking down class assignments into smaller pieces

For example, if the assignment was to complete 100 math problems, she would only have to complete 50. This would take her about the same amount of time as it would take a typical student to complete 100 problems, and it would allow her to finish the assignment to the best of her ability without getting frustrated.

I made it clear that I wasn't asking for her to receive less work; I was asking for her to have the best opportunity to complete the work, grasp the concepts, and be successful. Without these accommodations,

I was concerned that she would spiral into a negative space where she would feel unintelligent, lacking, and less than her peers. I was adamant about avoiding those feelings for her at all costs. I also made sure her educators knew how strong her work ethic was. Finally, I wanted to ensure that she wasn't penalized for these accommodations, since it was documented that her brain was functioning and processing information differently.

The Benefits of an IEP

One of the benefits of having an IEP in place is that it follows the person wherever they go. This means that if a person has IEP accommodations implemented in kindergarten, those accommodations should continue to be provided throughout their academic and employment careers.

I was so thankful to have finally put my daughter's IEP in place. From time to time, I would work with her educators to review and tweak the IEP to make sure it was meeting her needs. When she reached high school, one of the accommodations we added was for her to receive a copy of all assignments written on the board at the beginning of the day in every classroom. This way, she didn't have to worry about trying to write everything down at the same pace as her peers, and she was less likely to miss any important information.

Unfortunately, there are too many people in our society who view having an IEP as a detriment rather than a benefit. I used to think the same way. I have a friend who was diagnosed with ADHD. She works for the government at a well-known agency. Instead of making her employer aware of her diagnosis and the accommodations that would help her be successful, she chooses to suffer by remaining in a classroom taking an examination and staying at least three hours longer than her peers. She refuses to be labeled and to utilize the tools available to her. I have pleaded with her to make her employer aware of her IEP, but she would rather sit in silence for three additional hours after her peers have left to complete examinations. This seems like unnecessary suffering to me. I hope that after reading this book, she will take herself out of struggling mode and into thriving mode.

With the IEP in place, I noticed a significant improvement in my daughter's disposition. She was more confident and was beginning to like school again. She was given the assistance and support she needed, and she didn't have to constantly advocate for herself with her educators. Some of the pressure was removed, and she was able to focus on her learning.

Were you like I was? In denial? Frustrated? Losing hope? Not seeing a way out? Suffering alone? I want to encourage you! There IS a better way!

In the next chapter, I will share what happened six years after my daughter was diagnosed with ADHD.

Testimonial by Michelle Hibbert

Dr. Holmes is a great expert in her field. She was very thorough in explaining the process of the brain mapping and went through my results with great detail. I highly recommend her services.

CHAPTER 7

From Frustration to Freedom: Neurofeedback's Impact on Our Home

"Surrender to what is. Let go of what was.
Have faith in what will be."
Sonia Ricotti

I used to think that all hope was lost with my daughter being diagnosed with ADHD. It was her lot in life and nothing could be done about it. I now know that I was unequivocally and absolutely wrong... And I am so grateful!

I just happened to be reading through one of our Chiropractic magazines. There was an article that spoke about something called neurofeedback therapy. What grabbed my attention most from the article were the words that were in bold at the top. Non-invasive, drug-free therapy. ADHD, anxiety, depression. All I could think of was..."what was that and how did I get it"? Could it help my daughter? Drug free? Oh yes! I was all in! My eyes widened. What was THAT?!

After reading the article, there was a way to get more information about it for doctors. I immediately wrote the number down and decided to call them. I discovered that BrainCore is co-founded by one of my former Chiropractic professors, Dr. Guy Annunziata. He was looking for a solution to help his nephew who was diagnosed with Asperger's and came across neurofeedback therapy. Dr. Guy is a brilliant professor, so I knew he did his research before deciding to found a company regarding this remarkable therapy. I was pleased and thankful to know that someone I trusted was instrumental to the company. It gave me great hope and peace. Here was a possible solution that finally found me that could help change my daughter's life forever.

In chiropractic school, we are taught that chiropractic is first, drugs are second, and surgery is absolutely the last resort. I live by this philosophy, and I decided to apply it to this situation with my daughter. I was adamant about avoiding her taking medications at all. In my opinion, the side effects of medications are worse than what you are originally taking them for. I was not confident that the side effects would not affect my daughter as much as other people. The most common side effect of taking medications for attention deficit hyperactivity disorder is a loss of appetite. If you know my oldest daughter, then you know that she is lean and petite. She doesn't have anything to give so having her appetite decreased or lessened in any way was not an option.

After scheduling an interest meeting to discuss neurofeedback therapy and the possibility of becoming a practitioner, I prayed and decided to invest in an office system for my daughter. I purchased the entire system solely for my daughter. No one else mattered honestly. I was going to do whatever was necessary to help her. I didn't care how much it cost and I didn't know how I was going to purchase the system. I just knew that this was it and I needed to do it. So I did what any other parent would do. I found a way to make it happen.

I got trained and certified on the system and began her mental health journey one training session at a time. The first step was to have a qEEG brain mapping performed to assess how her brain was functioning. I came to understand that the qEEG brain mapping is the gold standard for neurofeedback analysis. It is the baseline from which all training sessions begin. Before BrainCore Neurofeedback Therapy, my daughter was having focus and attention issues. She was socially awkward, struggling in school academically, being socially bullied, and was taking about 5 hours each night to complete homework assignments. It was a nightmare that continued for 13 years. After working with me and the Dr. Holmes Method, she became the most focused student in class according to her teachers. She was so focused, she would get her peers back on task, I was told. She went from struggling in school to earning A's in honors chemistry and honors physics in high school. She went from being socially awkward and having very few friends, to trying out for the step and softball teams in high school and making both teams. She was no longer being bullied. She had many friends and became a social butterfly. She was finally getting the social cues! Her confidence soared and she was being invited to social events and was confident going and participating in all the high school activities that were offered. She went from taking approximately 5 hours each night to complete her homework assignments to now only two and a half to three hours.

One day, my mother-in-law called. Even though I'm divorced, I still call her my mother-in-law. I am very thankful that my in-laws are still in-laws and not outlaws as I've heard when the relationship that brought the family together has dissolved. When a marriage has ended and a divorce has occurred, I have heard former in-laws being referred to as outlaws. That is not the case in this situation, thank God! My mother-in-law said, "Now she has just blossomed into herself, hasn't she?!" I told her "YES she has! Thank you, God, and thank you neurofeedback!" That's the only thing that changed. My youngest daughter one day told me her observation and said, "You know what Mommy? You don't yell at her like you used to." My face went into shock mode. I was yelling at her out of frustration. I had worked all day, come home to my second job at around 7:00 every night during the week and would have to sit up and help her with homework to get it completed until midnight every single night. I was tired. And when I'm tired as most of us are as parents, we are not the most patient. I had become a yeller. I didn't want to. But I did. That was one of the things that I'm most proud of is that the whole home environment and stress levels in our home changed significantly after working with my daughter with the therapy. It single-handedly changed the trajectory of our household and all our lives were positively affected by its results. Again, I'm so thankful!

This therapy works to retrain how the brain functions. When the brain is functioning in a dysregulated or less efficient way, then a person develops symptoms such as anxious thoughts, focus and attention issues, depressed moods, poor sleep, headaches, and so on as a result. When my daughter had her initial brain mapping performed, it was discovered that the probability that her brain experiencing delta theta dysregulation, which is associated with focus on attention issues, impulsivity, and excessive speech was at 100%. The probability that her brain was experiencing beta dysregulation was around 82%. The probability that her brain was experiencing Alpha dysregulation was around 42%. Beta dysregulation is associated with panic attacks, worrying, and the like. Alpha dysregulation is associated with depressed moods, anger, and the like. Her cognitive dysregulation, which is a combination of the Delta, Theta, Beta, and Alpha dysregulations was at 100%. THAT'S why my baby was struggling academically! A neurotypical brain has less than 20% dysregulation. With her first brain mapping, all three categories of dysregulation were well over 20%. Seeing just how much her brain was not functioning well in black and white in that report was eye-opening! With the BrainCore system, the goal is for the dysregulation categories to have readings below 20%. Any dysregulation category above 20% is a cause for concern. After I saw her report, all I could do was focus on how many times I yelled at her and was frustrated with her and lacked patience. I was very disappointed with myself. I had to remind myself that I did the best that I could with what I knew at that time. Now that I knew better, I would do better.

The Journal of Medicine and Life: 2020 Jan-Mar: 13(1): 8-15, states, "Quantitative electroencephalography (QEEG) is a modern type of electroencephalography (EEG)" and is a useful clinical tool with extensive applications. According to the Journal of Occupational Health 2020 Jan-Dec; 62(1): e12121, Delta brainwave frequency is 0 to 4 hertz (HZ). It is the lowest frequency and is associated with dreamless sleep. In infants, it is the most dominant until approximately age one. Most people with focus and attention challenges tend to naturally increase delta wave activity when trying to focus rather than decrease it. Theta brainwave frequency is from 4 to 8 HZ and is associated with creativity, daydreaming, and intuition. Theta brainwaves are strong during meditation, prayer, spiritual awareness, and internal focus. It is believed to reflect the activity of the limbic system. Alpha brainwave frequency is in the 8 to 13 HZ range and is associated with a wakefulness state. Have you ever felt like you were "in the zone" when completing a task? You were so efficient and completed the task with ease and relaxation? You were most likely in the alpha state. It is described as being the bridge between the conscious and the subconscious. A normal asymmetry of alpha occurs in the brain with more located on the right side of the brain than on the left side. It is significant to the dysregulation patterns found in brain mapping reports. Beta brain wave frequency is the fastest and is in the 13 to 20 HZ range. They are activated and processed in the cortex of the brain. In this frequency, analytical problem solving, decision making, processing information, and making judgements regarding the world around us is dominant. There is also a normal asymmetry with beta with more located on the left side of the brain then on the right side of the brain. In my practice, an objective assessment comes before a patient's qEEG brain mapping. The results of the brain mapping are compared to the normative database and demonstrate how well the brain is functioning according to the patient's presenting symptoms, age, and clinical, and family history. The BrainCore System has a series of questions that provides a screening of the patient's metabolic functioning. This will be used to determine whether the patient's case is straightforward or more complex.

In my daughter's case, the objective findings dictated that her case was more straightforward. However, due to the fact that the brainwave dysfunction categories were over 20%, the program I recommended would require a greater amount of time and training sessions. On average, typical neurofeedback therapy patients would expect to see results after approximately 30 sessions or more.

At that time, I would bring my daughter into my office twice a week. Looking back, I realize I was not as consistent with her as I was with my other patients. There would be times when she would not be taken to the office to have training sessions for weeks at a time, unfortunately. Life happens. She might have had to complete an assignment at school or an extracurricular activity that would fill up that time. The training sessions last thirty minutes each. During the training, the patient is connected to the computer with non-invasive sensors. When the brain is in the brainwave frequency that we are trying to assist, then the patient sees the television program or movie they are watching nicely and brightly, and they hear it well. When the brain starts going into the undesired frequency, then the screen starts to fade like the dimmer on a light switch and the volume decreases. This is what I call an undesired consequence. The best thing about this is the negative consequences don't hurt. The entire therapy process is non-invasive, drug-free, scientific, modern, and effective. A complete game-changer!

I remember when my daughter would get upset with me when her movie wasn't over in thirty minutes. She wanted to continue watching her full movie or television show. The best aspect of the therapy was being able to watch thirty minutes of her favorite movies and shows uninterrupted. I wasn't on her about watching too much television. It was screen time that was beneficial for her brain! With neurofeedback therapy, at least four hours of rest are required for the brain before beginning another training session. As a result, we would leave the office and go to the park or shopping or do something else during that four-hour resting period. We would then return and pick up right where she left off.

Great work you got through all the scientific information that most people will skip through! Not you though! You're in it to win it/for the long haul!

Next, I'll share the results of my daughter's follow-up qEEG results and several sessions over several months.

Testimonial by Chelsea Munhall

I had been experiencing higher anxiety than in the past and wanted to try something new to me. Neurofeedback has helped me to feel calmer. I have the ability to pause and not react to negative experiences so quickly. I know to pause but I was having trouble pausing and taking time to respond before reacting. I'm grateful to Dr. Holmes for providing a solution for my anxiety that did not involve medication.

CHAPTER 8

Unlocking the Potential:
The Journey to Transformation

"We cannot change the cards we are dealt, just how we play the hand."
Randy Pausch

Making lasting changes in the brain would be difficult and time-consuming, is what I used to think before coming across neurofeedback therapy. Now, I know more regarding the brain's ability to adapt and change rapidly.

One of the things I love most about neurofeedback therapy is how easy it is!

Before I had home units to rent to my patients, I exclusively saw them in my office. Parents would often tell me that if their child(ren) asked one more time if they were going to therapy that day, they wouldn't be able to take it anymore. I would laugh! How great is it when children are genuinely excited to go to therapy?

I once had a patient in his sixties who came to me because he was having ticks and other challenges and was concerned about his ability to continue working well into his late seventies and early eighties. He began working with me in one of my programs, and after his third session, he asked when we were going to start the training.

"That was your third session!" I said.

"I thought you said the screen was going to fade," he replied.

"It went completely black three times!" I replied. "Didn't you see that?"

"No," he said.

At his next appointment, I decided to use his phone to record his session so he could pay attention to the screen fading in and out. I set up the tripod and connected his phone to record the training session. After he completed the session, I asked if he noticed the fading in and fading out of the screen. He did not. I then removed his phone from the tripod and showed the recording to him. It was only then that he was able to view the fading in and out of the screen. The fading was so subtle to him that it went unnoticed. It's that easy. There's no need to mentally strain to bring about a desired result.

Now, the ability to use home neurofeedback therapy units is a reality. With the addition of home units to my practice, I am able to monitor my patients' sessions remotely. Adding home units to my practice has been a significant and helpful development, as it allows patients to complete more training sessions in a shorter amount of time. It's also more convenient for my patients to have the ability to complete training sessions on their own schedule, rather than having to coordinate with mine. If they are night owls and want to complete a 30-minute session at home at 10:00 p.m., then they can.

Over the course of the next few months, my daughter completed multiple neurofeedback training sessions. It was finally time for her next qEEG brain mapping. One of the best aspects of the BrainCore System is that with follow-up brain mappings, the computer compares the most recent brain mapping to the one prior by tracking the patient's percentage of progress towards normalization.

I was amazed at my daughter's results! She went from having a 100% probability of Delta Theta dysregulation to under 20% in her second brain mapping. She went from having an 85% probability of Beta dysregulation to under 40%. She went from a 42% probability that her brain was experiencing Alpha dysregulation to 20%. Her cognitive dysregulation went from 100% probability to just under 80%. Cognitive dysregulation is a combination of Delta Theta, Alpha, and Beta dysregulations. It is favorable and desired to have or to be under 20% for all dysregulations.

If neurofeedback therapy could transform my child, then what could it do for other children and people who are suffering and struggling with challenges such as hers and yet do not know neurofeedback therapy exists? That's when my vision started to expand to what neurofeedback therapy could do for others outside of my family.

That's when it clicked for me: The public needed to know about this life-changing therapy! What could I do? How could I go about getting this message out?

As time went on, I noticed a significant decrease in my agitation towards my daughter. Our household became a happier, more joyous, and more peaceful place to be. My youngest daughter remarked how I no longer screamed at her sister. In my exhaustion, I became a yeller, unfortunately.

I vividly recall the times when my daughter would apologize profusely for having ADHD and for the frustration and overwhelm, she and our family endured. In retrospect, I realized that my daughter's ADHD diagnosis was a blessing in disguise. If it hadn't been for that diagnosis, we would never have discovered the transformative power of neurofeedback therapy.

Neurofeedback proved to be the key to transforming how our family lived and functioned.

With sixteen years of experience as a chiropractor, I was already established in my field when my daughter received an ADHD diagnosis. Witnessing the transformative impact of neurofeedback therapy on her life, inspired me to incorporate it into my practice. It was a seamless integration. As chiropractors, we are drawn to non-invasive, drug-free approaches, and our focus lies in the intricate workings of the nervous system. Coincidentally, the nervous system, which governs every aspect of our bodies, is encased within the spinal column. While many perceive chiropractors as solely focused on bone adjustments, our primary objective is to perform spinal adjustments to rectify nerve impingements or spinal subluxations, enabling the body to function optimally. When the nervous system operates at peak capacity, the body experiences enhanced health, a more robust immune system, and a state free from pain.

The brain and spinal cord form the core components of the nervous system.

Neurofeedback therapy offers a unique opportunity to directly induce positive changes within the brain. The question I frequently encounter is, "What sparked your decision to pursue this therapy?" Once I explain the inherent connection between chiropractors' focus on the nervous system and neurofeedback therapy, the concept becomes instantly clear.

In the next chapter, I have shared some of the fantastic case studies of the patients I have had the pleasure of caring for in my practice. Witness firsthand the powerful and inspiring transformations they have experienced with BrainCore Neurofeedback Therapy.

Testimonial by Dr. Muriel Thibodeaux, Ed.D.

I had my doubts about whether Neurofeedback would work. She explained to me how it works and how it would make a difference in my life.

After completing an 8-week session, I can say that I rest-assured that Neurofeedback has completely changed my life and has helped me improve my coping skills to manage my daily challenges better. After working with Dr. Holmes, I noticed that my speech is clearer, my cognitive problems are diminishing, my memory is clearer, I can concentrate more easily, and I can read a book for longer than 10 minutes! I am completely focused and can accomplish more in less time now than I ever have been. I can do anything whenever I want, and most importantly, I feel happy again. It has helped me become more focused and much more patient. Even my husband commented that my emotional rollercoaster ride had come to an end after the first four weeks into the program. I cannot describe how grateful and appreciative I am to Dr. Holmes for this! She has been a Godsend! I am so lucky! With her help, I was able to regain my life, independence, and overall well-being. With this review, I want to be an inspiration for those suffering from a brain injury. I highly recommend considering Neurofeedback as an option for not just your brain, but for your peace of mind.

CHAPTER 9

Revealing Transformations: Real Stories of Triumph

"You never change your life until you step out of your comfort zone; Change begins at the end of your comfort zone."
Roy T. Bennett

T
his collection presents a selection of case studies and patient experiences from my practice. These real-life stories highlight the transformative power of neurofeedback therapy and its ability to positively impact individuals' lives.

Beyond Migraines: The Unforeseen Benefits of Neurofeedback

When my children were younger, they would go to the Boys & Girls Club after school. I noticed a woman who looked very familiar to me from an event I attended earlier at another location. At the Boys & Girls Club, I went up to her and told her that she looked familiar. Eventually, we were able to determine where we knew each other from. It turns out that her son and my daughters attended a children's event together at a school fair. We began chatting it up and

I found we had similar interests. We later began notifying each other of events and activities where our children could make new friends, learn, and have fun.

As our friendship grew, she began sharing with me how she had been having migraine headaches daily since her father passed away. I immediately said, "Well, that's not normal." She said no, it wasn't, but it's been my normal for the past few years. It was at that time I shared with her about the therapy that helped my daughter. I explained how neurofeedback therapy works to get her brain waves to regulate themselves and the probability that she would no longer have the symptoms of migraine headaches after completing one of my programs. She was a single mom like I was and was unable to make the investment into one of my programs at that time. At another Neurofeedback conference, it was mentioned how some offices selected scholarship patients. These were patients who were offered neurofeedback therapy completely free of charge.

Here was an opportunity for me to help my friend and to also gain more practice with helping a patient with migraine headaches. I offered to help her with my neurofeedback therapy program by offering it to her as one of my first scholarship patients. She was thrilled and was so appreciative!

I gathered information about her history, including when she first started experiencing migraine headaches. I then scheduled her first qEEG brain mapping appointment. Before the appointment, she completed questionnaires, including a metabolic processes screening to ensure they were functioning well. This is an important factor because it affects how well the brain responds to and changes with therapy. Pre-appointment instructions and recommendations include getting plenty of rest, drinking water, and avoiding recreational drugs. Patients are also reminded to only use shampoo on their hair before the brain mapping, as hair products can coat the hair follicle and affect the results.

The brain mapping procedure is non-invasive, drug-free, and takes approximately 45 to 60 minutes to complete. It assesses how the brain is functioning. The patient wears a fitted cap with sensors that harness brain waves for the report. Children as young as 5 years old can easily have brain mappings performed. Half of the brain mapping is done with the patient's eyes closed and the other half with the patient's eyes open. This is because the brain behaves differently when the eyes are open versus closed. When the eyes are open, the brain focuses on goal-oriented tasks and the environment; when the eyes are closed, the brain tends to wander freely and is more meditative. Understanding these neurological shifts helps me tailor my neurofeedback programs to various mental health and wellness challenges.

After the brain mapping, the patient schedules another appointment to review the findings. It is helpful for the patient to bring a family member, spouse, or significant other to this appointment to help remember the details and answer any questions.

After presenting the report of findings, I gave my patient a program recommendation based on the results of the brain mapping. Her program consisted of three visits per week until her brain adapted to the assigned protocol.

Neurofeedback therapy is a modality that essentially exercises the brain to teach it how to regulate itself during training sessions. Each session lasts thirty minutes, during which the patient is connected to a computer using sensors placed on their scalp at the locations determined by the report. The primary location is addressed first.

The patient watches a movie, television show, or video on a streaming device. The device's screen and volume either brighten and increase or dim and decrease depending on the brain's ability to adapt and change.

When the brain is operating well at the target frequency, the patient sees and hears the video clearly. When the brain goes into a dysfunctional frequency, the screen fades and the volume decreases. This is called *operant conditioning*, a type of positive and negative reinforcement. In this case, the negative reinforcement is not painful, but simply entails the volume decreasing and the screen getting darker or fading. Concentration is not necessary during therapy, and the overall effort required is minimal.

I was unaware that watching comedy shows during neurofeedback training sessions is discouraged. I learned this at a symposium I attended. People tend to move when they laugh, which can displace the sensors on their scalp and require the practitioner to pause the session to reset them.

After learning of this caveat, I informed my patients that they should not watch comedies during their sessions. This is disappointing, as I believe laughter is the best medicine.

One of my patients was watching a comedy show in my office early one morning during her training session. She was laughing so hard that I wrote down the name of the show so I could watch it later myself. Thankfully, her sensors remained attached.

After analyzing her training sessions for a couple of months, I noticed that her brainwave frequency was normalizing. This meant it was time for her follow-up brain mapping.

I asked her if she had noticed any differences or changes after about the fifteenth session. (This varies for each patient.)

She said, "Oh yes, I'm not having migraines anymore!"

I said, "What? You forgot to tell me this? The main reason you came in to see me and you forgot to tell me this?"

She started laughing. "Oh, Doc," she said. "That's not what I noticed the most."

She proceeded to tell me that she was taking college courses. It used to take her about 3 to 4 hours to complete homework assignments, because she would have difficulty understanding and remembering what she read. Now, since working with me and my program, it only took her about 2 hours to complete her homework every night. She is able to understand what she reads and immediately answer the questions correctly and quickly without having to go back. This allows her to have more time with her children rather than having her head buried in a book completing homework until it's time for them to go to bed.

I told her that is what I call a positive side effect. Neurofeedback therapy is not only for those who are having mental health challenges, but also for optimal brain performance and stress relief. I've had executives in corporations who sought my programs to help ensure they could continue working into their 70s and 80s. They wanted to maintain or enhance mental sharpness while preventing mental decline. That's the power of neurofeedback therapy!

I have added a key to help you understand the brain function graphs that follow after each patient's journey. Below, you will find a legend that explains the numbers on the graphs, illustrating the brain's functionality before and after neurofeedback therapy.

Legend:

Most Dysregulated: Areas of the brain the therapy will focus on primarily.

Number	Brain Function
0-2	Well-functioning/Optimal
2-10	Dysfunctional/Suboptimal (indicates need for neurofeedback therapy)

Image 1A

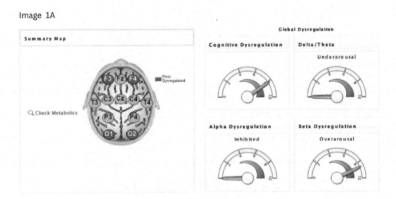

Image 1B

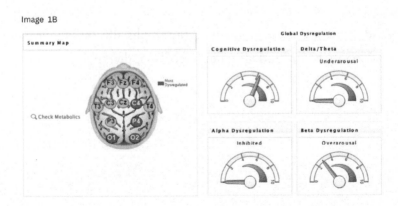

Empowering the Future: A Proactive Approach to Brain Health

One day, I received a call from a 29-year-old woman who was concerned about her brain. Her mother had been diagnosed with frontotemporal dementia at 50 years old, and she was worried that she might develop the same condition. She told me that she had been having challenges at work with remembering numbers and completing tasks, which alarmed her. She was married with two young sons and did not want them to have to care for her the way she and her brother had to care for their mother. She wanted to be proactive rather than reactive, and that's why she called my office.

I invited her to come in for her first brain mapping session after gathering all the pertinent history documentation. The brain mapping report showed different levels of brain activity. I went over the report with her and explained that she was a candidate to begin one of my neurofeedback programs. I told her what to expect while in training and what the benefits were for patients who participated in my programs.

After beginning my program, the patient noticed significant changes in her memory, efficiency, and work performance. She no longer had difficulty transposing or remembering numbers, and she was able to complete her job duties without having to meticulously write and take notes. This saved her a significant amount of time and allowed her to focus on other tasks.

She was grateful for the positive impact of neurofeedback therapy on her life and her children's future. She realized that they would likely not have to care for her in the same way that she and her brother were caring for their mother. She was determined to provide her sons with the freedom to live their own lives.

She understood the importance of early detection and intervention, and she was thankful for the opportunity to improve her quality of life.

Image 2A

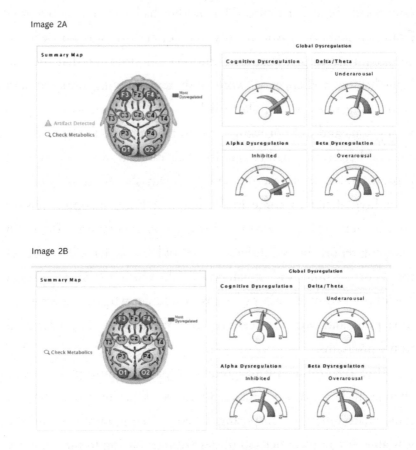

Image 2B

Unlocking Academic Success: A Teen's Triumph Over ADHD

A teenage boy was struggling in school, unable to focus and maintain attention in class. His mother called me, explaining that he had been diagnosed with ADHD. We discussed his situation, and she shared that he attended a very exclusive private school. His main issue was that he was failing every class except for physical education.

Understandably, his parents were not pleased. His mother told me she had to do something because her husband was so upset with their son's underperformance that he was ready to pull him out of school. He questioned why they should spend their hard-earned money if their son wasn't doing his part.

I asked if anyone else in their family had been diagnosed with ADHD. The mother admitted that she felt her husband was an undiagnosed adult with ADHD. She said no one in her family had the same diagnosis, and that her husband was in a bit of denial about their son's diagnosis. Perhaps this was because he saw the same challenges he had faced mirrored in his son. However, since the father had worked through his challenges, he felt his son could do the same without any help. He reasoned that he had figured it out, so why couldn't his son?

After completing the consultation, I learned that their son had suffered a concussion while playing football. He had been head-butted, and his focus, attention, and memory had suffered as a result. His memory was so poor that his father would become frustrated and upset with him for not being able to remember things. His mother knew she had to do something, as the relationship between her husband and their son was quickly deteriorating.

After his initial brain mapping, the son started my neurofeedback therapy program. At that time, patients came into my office two to three times a week for their training sessions. After a few weeks of training, I would typically ask my patients and their parents if they noticed any changes.

Initially, neither of them noticed any differences. However, one day, after asking the son if he was noticing anything, he said, "*You know what, Dr. Holmes? I was in my math class and the teacher was explaining the lesson. Typically, I would have trouble understanding what he was trying to teach us. However, after he taught this lesson, I immediately understood what he was teaching. It's like something clicked. I was so happy to finally understand something! He gave us class work to complete, and I was able to complete it right away. I was even able to help some of my friends in class who were having trouble understanding the lesson. My teacher asked me what I was doing that was different. I told him some BrainCore thing. He said, "Keep it up!"*

The patient looked at me and said, "*You know what? You're onto something here! This stuff works!*" I said, "You think? Imagine what it would do if you were doing your homework?!" He laughed, knowing full well that he wasn't complying with my at-home requirements for entrainment exercises.

Entrainment exercises are a way for the brain to use visual and audible stimulation to train or exercise the brain to resonate at the same frequency pulses that are provided to the patient during a neurofeedback training session. When the brain shifts into the corresponding state of the brainwave frequencies that are involved with the AVE or audio-visual entrainment, then the result is an improved state of mind and performance. I would have my patients perform entrainment exercises on the days they did not come into the office so the gains that were made during the neurofeedback therapy session would be reinforced. The brain would make a shift into the proper or desired brain wave frequencies during the neurofeedback therapy session. That's why I called it homework. It only took 15 to 20 minutes, so it wasn't too long of an assignment.

The young man completed his program at my office and school was coming to a close for the summer. I told him I wanted to be kept abreast of his grades and what his final ones were at the end of the semester. I was fully invested in his academic results. I followed up with his mother approximately one week after school let out to get a tally of his final grades. He ended up passing every class! I asked what the percentage was that he earned in his math class, and she said that he earned 88%. I so wanted him to earn a 90 or above so that he could earn that A and I told her as much. She laughed and said that she and her husband were very thrilled and excited he was able to pull his grades up and the only reason that happened must have been because of the program he completed at my office. That was the only thing that changed during their son's daily routine. *"Now,"* she said, *"if I could just get my husband on your program!"* We both laughed. I said, "I'll be here when he's ready!"

Image 3A

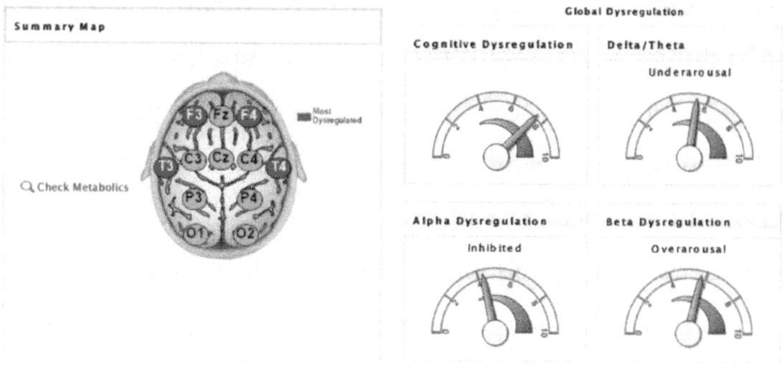

Image 3B

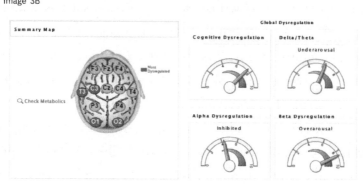

Reclaiming Her Mind:
A Doctor's Journey from Cognitive
Struggles to Achievement

At a holiday networking event a few years ago, I met a doctor with a doctorate in education. We were talking and naturally, she asked me what I did. I shared what I offer to my patients and community, and she was intrigued. She told me how she had suffered major injuries in a horrific car accident a year or so earlier, and I encouraged her to reach out to me to see if neurofeedback therapy could help. She said she would.

I would see her at other networking events after we first met, and we would chat briefly. I would never mention her contacting me. My thoughts are geared toward understanding how people will contact you when they are ready to change what's going on in their lives. When they are ready to begin, I'm ready to assist them on their mental health and wellness journey.

Two years passed, and while speaking with the doctor, I noticed that it was taking her longer and longer to come up with the words she was trying to express during our conversation. It was like she was talking in slow motion. Her speech and conversational skills were much worse than when we first met. I asked how she was doing, and she said that she too had noticed herself going further and further downhill cognitively. I reminded her that my office was still open.

The following week, she called my office and shared more extensive details about her car accident and injuries. She was having trouble concentrating and focusing, was easily distracted, and found it difficult to recall information at times. She said her symptoms varied from day to day, but on average, she rated her severity as an eight on a scale of one to ten, with one being no severity and ten being high severity. She was unable to perform her duties as an educator because of her lack of focus and difficulty recalling information for each student. She had to resign from that position. She said she was constantly on information overload and that the stress was too hard to manage. She said she had never been medically diagnosed with a concussion from the car accident, but she told me how her car had flipped several times and hit a cement partition, and how a tire iron had come through the windshield and grazed her right temple. She suspected that she had suffered a concussion.

Her initial online paperwork hinted at high levels of brain inflammation and abnormally high levels of attention and impulsivity. After her initial brain mapping, I invited her husband to join the report of findings, where I went over the details of the report and explained and demonstrated where her brain was functioning well and not so well. Based on the results of the brain mapping, I recommended the program that was best for her. Thankfully, at that time in my practice, I had added the use of home units for my programs. I recommended that she rent one of my home units so she could perform the brain training sessions in the comfort and convenience of her home. This would allow her to get better results faster simply because she could perform the training sessions on demand, without having to worry about coordinating schedules with me. She and her husband agreed to begin the program.

Typically, I follow up with my patients and congratulate them on completing their first training session. This confirms to them that I am monitoring their sessions and that I know what they have accomplished. After congratulating her on completing her initial session, I followed up with her approximately a week later.

Initially, she and her husband were concerned about the investment in the program if it did not work for her. I had recommended the program for severe and complicated cases, but they wanted to only commit to the program I recommended for mild, uncomplicated cases. I agreed to allow them this option, as I understood that this was new territory for them.

After a week of beginning the home unit program, I asked her how things were going and if she had noticed any changes yet. She said she was so glad I asked! She reported sleeping better, having less frustration and more patience, and her children were no longer "getting on her nerves." She was able to wake up at a decent time of day and was no. She was no longer sluggish and sleeping all day long. She also shared with me how she was back to writing again. Before the motor vehicle accident that caused her current issues, she had written articles that were published in various educational journals. I expressed how happy I was for her! I also reminded her that she was only working on 1/4 of the program I recommended, and imagined what would happen if she completed the entire program. Immediately, she told me how she and her husband had already discussed how they were ready to complete the entire program.

It was now time for the doctor's follow-up qEEG brain mapping. Her husband accompanied her to the appointment, and he told me almost immediately after coming into my office that he didn't even need her to have another brain mapping because he had his wife back. He said he saw her coming back to herself and was over-the-moon thankful that she was getting back to her old self again.

Being the educated woman that she is, the doctor agreed that, yes, she was feeling better and knew she was getting better, but she still wanted to see the data. I laughed and told her I understood. I am a science lover, too!

As expected, her follow-up brain mapping showed tremendous improvements. The BrainCore system I use in my office has a comparison feature that objectively compares one brain mapping to another. After the computer compares the brain mappings, a percentage towards normalization is calculated. Ideally, we would like this percentage to be 20% or more. This demonstrates how the brain is being transformed effectively through the use of neurofeedback.

The doctor's percentage towards normalization achieved with her eyes closed was 35%. The percentage towards normalization that was achieved with her eyes opened was 64%. Both percentages were well over 20%. We all high-fived each other. That provided the documentation and objective findings demonstrating my program's effectiveness.

The doctor had tears in her eyes and thanked me for not nagging and hassling her to give me a call all the times our paths crossed years earlier. She was kicking herself because she waited so long to make that call to me. If only she had called me soon after she met me, she would have saved herself and her family over two years of frustration and disappointment. The strain on her marriage would have been lifted, and so forth and so on.

I understood and shared how everything happens as it should. Everything happens at the time it is supposed to happen. I was just thankful we were placed together at that time so many years ago, so she could at least benefit from this life-changing, drug-free, non-invasive, and effective therapy.

Since completing her program at my office, the doctor has resumed writing and has finished writing her book! She is back to being the involved and caring wife, mother, educator, entrepreneur, and friend that she was, prior to the accident.

Thank you, neurofeedback therapy!

Image 4A

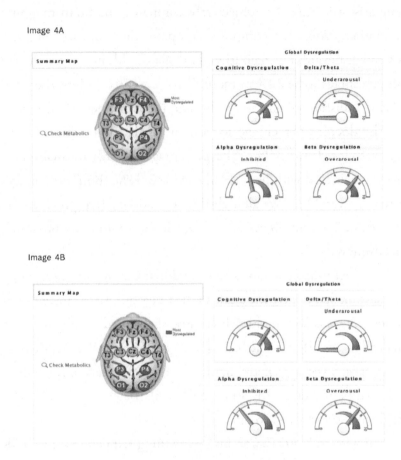

Image 4B

Home Runs and Happiness: Overcoming Childhood Anxiety

A concerned mother called my office to discuss her 8-year-old son's extreme anxiety. He had been experiencing crying fits, refusing to go to school or participate in sports or activities, and having stomach aches for the past five months. He also had a fear of choking, regurgitating, getting sick, death, and separation anxiety.

His symptoms had escalated almost to the point of debilitation in the three weeks leading up to his mother's call. She rated their severity as 8 out of 10. She shared how her son had lost interest in his usual activities and had very little joy. He had been an avid baseball player, dreaming of playing professionally in the Major League Baseball Association, but he could no longer enjoy the game.

When I asked if she could relate his symptoms to any past event, she mentioned that he had regurgitated while at a sleepover, and that his anxiety had intensified after that. He had been diagnosed with anxiety and panic disorder by a therapist.

After asking more questions, I discovered that his father also suffered from anxious thoughts and had been on medication for years. The mother did not want her son to rely on medication as her husband did. She wanted his future to look different. That's why she called me.

After completing the preliminary online questionnaires, the patient's mother reported that he had been suffering from headaches, poor sleep, frequent stomach pains, and irritability when he missed meals. When I asked her about the missed meals, she told me that he refused to eat the food at school, resulting in long stretches of time between meals. She also said that he had gone so far as refusing to go to baseball practice, which he loved. This is when she knew something had to be done, as she felt like he was slipping away from her.

His initial brain mapping revealed dysregulation in all brain wave categories. This resulted in symptoms such as challenges with decision making, reading comprehension, math comprehension, impulsivity, and social inappropriateness. He was also hyper-emotional, easily distracted, passive-aggressive, angry, and struggled with ruminating and worrying.

After approximately 30 sessions, a follow-up brain mapping was performed. This comparison report showed a 27% total change towards normalization with his eyes closed and a 35% total change towards normalization with his eyes opened. His mother noticed some positive changes in his behavior, such as eating at school and no longer crying to go to school in the morning. He was also interested in playing baseball again and was excited to go to both practices and weekend tournaments with his travel team. The patient himself reported that he was able to sit still better.

His mother contacted me a couple of months after completing my program to thank me again. She was at an indoor play place with her son and daughter, where he had experienced a full-blown panic attack the last time they were there. *"Today, he's just a regular kid,"* she said. *"He's playing, eating, drinking, and simply enjoying himself without hesitation."* She was so happy, she could cry. She thanked me again, saying that she felt like a broken record because she kept pointing out how "normal" he was now. Her *"kiddo was back to himself again."* She recalled how they had gone to a family reunion the week before, and no one else knew, but she was in awe of how he had eaten random foods, met new cousins and friends, and played until he couldn't play anymore. He was finally back to being her son again. *"It was beautiful!"* she exclaimed.

Image 5A

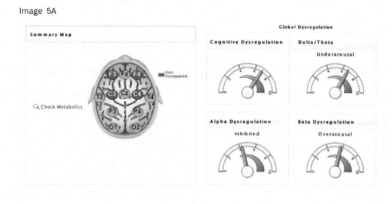

Image 5B

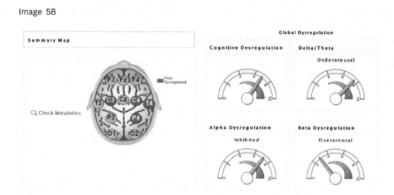

Awakening from Sleep Troubles:
A Journey to Renewed Vitality

A woman in poor health contacted me. During our consultation, she shared that she had been having trouble sleeping for the past six months, rating her symptom as an 8 out of 10 on the severity scale. I asked if she could relate her symptoms to any past events, and she mentioned running into a wood beam at a jungle gym when she was about seven years old. She also played soccer at the time, but no doctor confirmed that she had suffered a concussion or traumatic brain injury. She was certain, however, that she had suffered one of these injuries.

She handed me a list of her medications, which included ten medications, many of which had side effects that were worse than the conditions they were being treated for. She also completed the online paperwork, and the results of her metabolic screening placed her in the category of a more complicated case. The way our bodies metabolize hormones is a factor in brain health and how well the brain responds to any therapies, including neurofeedback therapy. Gathering this data is an important factor in determining the next steps to take for my patients. Her score from the screening was so high that I had to ask when the last time was she had her hormones checked. She answered that it might have been approximately two years since she had a physical.

With cases such as hers, I typically refer patients to a functional medicine doctor who specializes in endocrinology for an assessment. That way, patients have the option to use more natural methods for hormone regulation. I made that recommendation to her.

She began one of my neurofeedback programs. Prior to working with me, she told me that she only slept two hours each night. After the first two sessions, I asked if her sleep was improving. She was excited to share that it was, and that she was now sleeping four hours a night.

At the beginning of her next few sessions, I asked the same question and she reported that her sleep was continuing to improve greatly. She went from sleeping five hours a night to seven hours a night, then nine hours a night, and then eleven hours a night. She said, "*I feel like a completely different person!*"

I told her that she was truly sleeping now. She is not a machine, and our bodies require time to reset, restore, and replenish each day.

We all know what happens when we don't shut down our cell phones after a while. They act slowly and sluggishly. Maintaining a healthy sleeping routine of at least seven hours each night provides our brains and bodies with the opportunity to replenish, refresh, and restore.

I was grateful that she felt like a new person after the relatively small number of training sessions she completed.

When she first contacted me, she was in the midst of planning her wedding. Later, she sent me her wedding pictures. She looked fabulous, happy, and well-rested! She had no bags under her eyes, and she truly looked like a new person. She was glowing! Another win for neurofeedback!

Please note: This patient did not return for a follow-up brain mapping.

Image 6

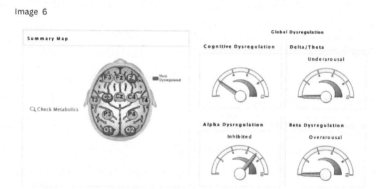

From Isolation to Interaction: The Remarkable Impact of Neurofeedback on Asperger's

A mother contacted me about her 14-year-old daughter, who had been diagnosed with Asperger's, a form of autism spectrum disorder (ASD). She was highly functioning but struggled with social skills. She would not interact with the public or even her extended family at gatherings, which was disheartening for her parents. They wanted her to experience the bond that family members share, but instead, she kept to herself.

Another challenge was anger. Her mother described her daughter's short fuse, citing examples such as getting upset if the mother took a different route to a weekly event or changed her daily routine. These were the challenges that the mother hoped to address with neurofeedback.

The mother also mentioned that her daughter had learning and memory challenges. I informed her that with certain conditions such as Asperger's/autism, the brain may require two to three times as long to respond to neurofeedback therapy. A typical patient would start to notice changes after approximately 15 to 20 sessions, but someone with ASD may need 30 or more sessions before seeing any noticeable results. She was undeterred.

At the time, training sessions could only be done in the office, so her mother brought her in, two to three times a week. Even though I knew it would take longer for her brain to show results and transformations, I was still hopeful that she would make progress sooner than expected.

One day, her mother came into my office. She usually went to the conference room to work on her laptop while her daughter was in training, but on this particular day, she came in to share some news. I was a bit concerned, as this was a drastic break from their normal routine.

She said, "*Guess what, Dr. Holmes? We had a family gathering this past weekend, and [her daughter] interacted with her aunts, uncles, and cousins!*" She explained that it was so noticeable that many of her relatives sought her out and expressed their delight. They were so elated to see how social and interactive her daughter was. They had never experienced this before.

A few days later, the mother told me that their plans had suddenly changed that day. She called her daughter downstairs from her room to give her the update. After telling her daughter what was changing, her daughter simply looked at her, said, "okay," and climbed the stairs to go back to her room. The mother said she was "in shock and her jaw hit the floor." She was so conditioned to and was waiting for the World War III reaction of rage and anger from her daughter that she didn't know how to respond when her daughter simply said, "okay," accepted the change, and went back up to her room. That was progress!

Image 7A

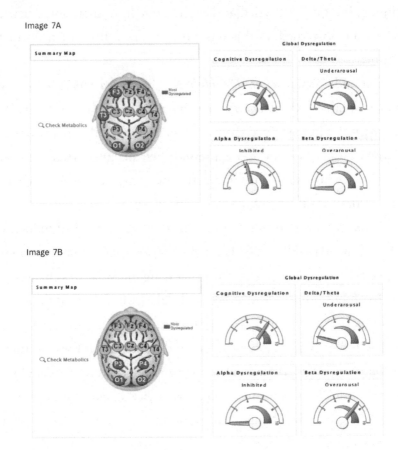

Image 7B

Silencing Stims: A Neurofeedback Approach to Nonverbal Autism Transformation

A mother of a 23-year-old son with autism spectrum disorder (ASD) contacted me. Her son was nonverbal, experienced over 20 stims daily, and had severe autism, anxiety, synesthesia, apraxia, and misophonia. He used a letter board to communicate and had fine motor skills, focusing, impulsivity, and misophonia difficulties. He also had issues on the right side of his body. His mother reported that he had telepathic and energy-sensing abilities, which is not uncommon in neurodivergent people.

He began my home unit program and completed over 90 training sessions. His mother understood that autistic brains typically take two to three times longer to respond to neurofeedback therapy than neurotypical brains. After four weeks, a follow-up brain mapping was performed.

After the brain mapping, I asked him if he noticed any differences compared to when he first came to my office. Using the letter board, he said that he now only experienced two to five stims per month, compared to over 20 per day. This outcome excited him the most. His comparison reports noted a 35% change towards normalization with his eyes closed and a 46% change towards normalization with his eyes open. Again, 20% or above is the goal we strive to achieve with comparison reports. He and his mother were pleased with the results and looked forward to returning to complete another program at another time.

Image 8A

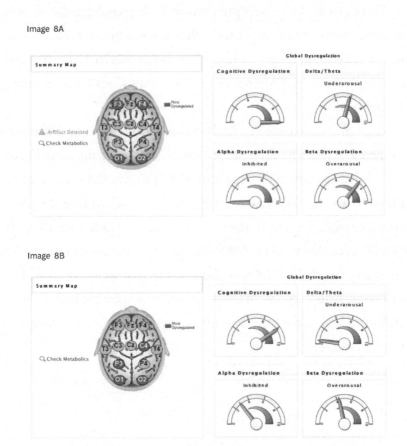

Image 8B

Rescue and Recovery: A Brave Journey through PTSD

A young woman moved to Georgia from another state and contacted my office to continue neurofeedback therapy that she had been receiving at a BrainCore office in her previous state. She reported suffering from severe PTSD, post-traumatic stress disorder. She had been in an abusive relationship with her ex-boyfriend, who had physically abused her, including throwing her headfirst against the wall. She could not estimate how many concussions or traumatic brain injuries she had suffered. The abuse had worsened to the point where she had to be rescued by the SWAT team.

She was dedicated to improving her mental health and came to my office five days a week for two straight weeks. I require that all my patients diagnosed with PTSD be under the care of a psychologist, counselor, or therapist during their neurofeedback program, so that they have resources available to them when triggers occur.

After a few weeks, I called her psychologist to check in and follow up. I was alarmed to learn that the therapist had not seen her in over a month, despite the patient telling me that her therapy sessions were going well. What she didn't know is that I am the queen of follow-up, and I am committed to providing my patients with the best possible care.

I immediately contacted her to remind her of my requirement to continue therapy with her mental health professional while partnering with me and receiving neurofeedback. She sheepishly admitted that she had not been in contact with her therapist. She said she had a new boyfriend and was spending a lot of time with him. I was concerned and asked her to confirm that her new boyfriend did not exhibit the same patterns as her ex. She assured me that he was a sweetheart and would never hurt her. I believed her, but I still stressed the importance of returning to therapy for the benefit of her therapist's years of training and experience.

Her parents visited town and requested to meet with me and attend one of her training sessions. They paid for her care. I agreed, as long as she was comfortable with it. She was in her 20s and had the right to admit or deny access to her parents.

During her next training session, my patient went into a full-blown episode. I looked at her parents, expecting them to spring into action as loving parents would. Instead, they sat there stoically, saying and doing nothing. I was shocked.

Since they weren't trying to console their daughter, I got up from my desk, sat next to her, and used a calming voice to let her know she was in a safe space, and everything was okay. It was the only thing I could think of doing. I knew better than to try to get in her personal space, even though my first instinct was to hug her. I wasn't sure how she would respond, and I didn't want to make matters worse. Thankfully, she came out of the episode of crying and trembling after about five minutes, even though it felt like an eternity.

My thoughts were focused on the fact that she had not had any triggers or episodes until her parents were present. Were they the cause of her PTSD? Was she nurtured as a child? Was the story of being rescued by the SWAT team from the abusive boyfriend a true experience? All these thoughts and questions ran through my mind.

She eventually decreased her training sessions to twice a week over the next few weeks. It was time to have a follow-up brain mapping performed.

Her results were outstanding! She experienced a 61% total change towards normalization with her eyes closed and a 59% total change towards normalization with her eyes open. These are phenomenal results. Unfortunately, her parents decided to end their financial support for her program, so she had to stop her care.

I continued to follow up with her even after she was no longer an active patient. She was grateful for my concern and told me that she had never had a doctor who took the time to see how she was doing after stopping care. On one of our calls, she told me that she was pregnant and excited about the future. She and her boyfriend were doing well, and everything was great. I was glad and relieved to hear it. It appeared that she was doing well, which is terrific!

What I remember the most about this patient is that when I first met her, she appeared to be the "all-American" young lady. She was beautiful, tall, blonde, and blue-eyed. She was unassuming and had a joyous, calming spirit. By looking at her, you would never know the tragedies she had experienced. Honestly, when she shared with me that she suffered from severe PTSD, I was taken aback. I thought to myself, "Really? Was she pulling my leg?" She wasn't. This is a reminder to never judge a book by its cover. Too often, we make assumptions about others solely based on their appearance. However, if we took the time to get to know someone and their experiences, most of us would never want to trade positions with them.

Image 9A

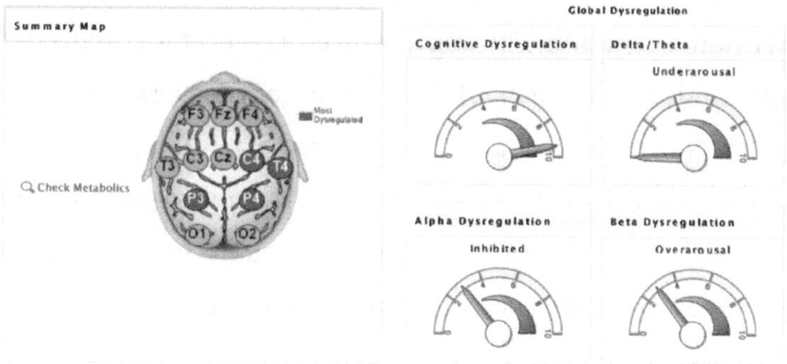

Image 9B

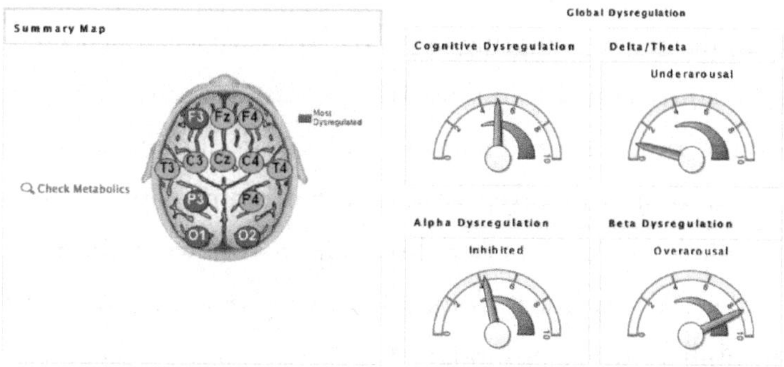

Empathy in Action:
Unraveling the Threads of Teenage Desperation

A call from the mother of a teenage daughter who had just been released three days prior from a suicide attempt sent a shockwave through me. My heart sank as I imagined the unimaginable pain and despair that must have driven her to such a desperate act. As a parent of two teenage daughters myself, I couldn't fathom the depth of suffering that could lead a young person to believe that ending their life was the only solution. The news struck a chord within me, stirring a torrent of emotions and a profound sense of empathy for this struggling family. Prayers immediately flooded my mind.

Without hesitation, I arranged a meeting with the parents to delve into the underlying causes of their daughter's distress and assess her suitability for neurofeedback therapy. The parents expressed a keen interest in exploring this non-pharmaceutical approach, having read, and researched its positive outcomes for many individuals. Their eagerness to find an alternative to medication resonated with my own belief in holistic healing.

After gathering more detailed information about the daughter's health history, I explained how her symptoms aligned with those of my typical patients. However, the most crucial factor was her willingness and commitment to engaging in the therapy. We scheduled a meeting with the entire family to discuss the process, ensuring that everyone was on the same page and ready to embark on this journey together.

The next step involved conducting a brain mapping to assess the daughter's brain functionality. Upon reviewing the results, I recommended my most comprehensive program, which offered the flexibility to accommodate her busy teenage schedule. The family wholeheartedly agreed, and the daughter embarked on her neurofeedback program.

Another valuable aspect of my system is the supplement section. The qEEG brain mapping often reveals deficiencies in vitamins and nutrients, and the daughter's report was no exception. I recommended whole-food supplements to address these imbalances, emphasizing the intricate connection between the gut and the brain, commonly known as the gut-brain axis. As Harvard Medical School aptly states, "the brain and the gastrointestinal (GI) system are intimately connected." (Harvard Health Publishing, The Gut-Brain Connection: July 18, 2023)

This connection often becomes evident when a patient's self-reported diet appears adequate, yet the brain mapping reveals a different story. It serves as a stark reminder of the profound impact of nutrition on our overall health and well-being.

After four weeks in my program, her brain mapping results indicated a remarkable 55% total change toward normalization with her eyes closed and a 36% total change with her eyes open. Her dedication to the program was evident, as she consistently completed two 30-minute training sessions daily, with a mandatory four-hour rest period between sessions. This rest period allows the brain to assimilate and adapt to the changes induced by each training session, a process facilitated by neuroplasticity, the brain's remarkable ability to form new neural pathways.

As soccer season approached, her mother expressed concern about her ability to maintain the two-session regimen. I reassured her that at this stage, one session per day would suffice, emphasizing the importance of outdoor activities, fresh air, vitamin D, and exercise, which would complement the training sessions and promote overall well-being. I also reminded her that sports and extracurricular activities promote socialization, a crucial aspect of teenage brain development.

Two weeks later, her mother called to report a noticeable change in her daughter's behavior. She was rolling her eyes and exhibiting more frequent moments of rudeness. "Oh," I responded, "so she's acting like a regular teenager?" Her mother couldn't help but chuckle. "Isn't that better than the alternative?" I added. Her mother wholeheartedly agreed, relieved to see her daughter exhibiting signs of typical teenage behavior.

Upon completing my program, the young athlete returned to her former self, actively participating in social activities, and resuming her soccer endeavors. When I inquired about her team's performance, she shared that they were doing well, but she wasn't a starter due to her perceived lack of skill. I reassured her that enjoying the game and participating were far more important than being a starter. "You're a teenager," I reminded her, "that's how it's supposed to be!" For the first time since starting the program, I witnessed a genuine smile grace her face. It was a moment of pure joy for me, and I commended her for her dedication and perseverance. I expressed my eagerness to follow her future endeavors, promising to stay connected.

Image 10A

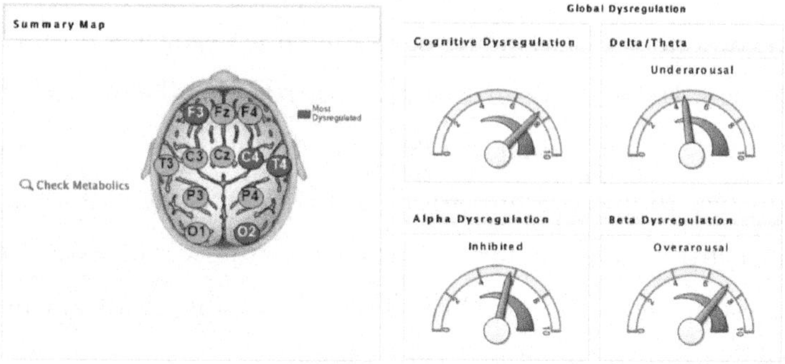

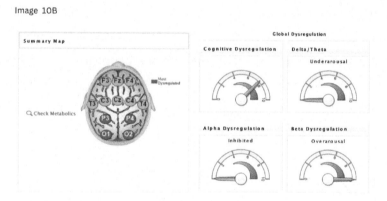

Image 10B

From Debilitation to Dominance: A Track Coach's Neurofeedback Odyssey to Athletic Glory and Beyond

I received a voicemail message from a gentleman inquiring about neurofeedback therapy. He mentioned being referred by a woman whose name I didn't recognize. I returned his call and scheduled a phone consultation. During our discussion, he revealed a history of continuous chronic headaches since October 2009, persisting until the present year, 2020. He had been diagnosed with new daily persistent headache, or NDPH, a condition I was unfamiliar with at the time.

He described experiencing daily migraine headaches, rating their severity as a 10 on a scale of 1 to 10, with 10 being the highest. Some migraines left him completely debilitated for 3 to 4 days, confining him to bed in a dark, cool room until the episode subsided. He couldn't attribute these headaches to any injuries, illnesses, or life traumas during the fall of 2009. The only notable event during that period was starting graphic design school.

I inquired about any history of concussions or traumatic brain injuries. He recalled a severe football accident in the 8th grade, during which he blacked out for about 15 to 20 seconds before regaining consciousness. Concussions weren't a major concern at the time, and baselines for diagnosis weren't established. He continued playing after the incident, believing it might have been a concussion, though it was never officially diagnosed.

I inquired about a brain MRI and was informed that he had one, with negative results. A brain MRI can detect tumors, inflammation, and injury-related damage. A negative result indicated the absence of these abnormalities. He mentioned consulting with various neurologists, but none could identify the cause of his headaches. He shared that his wife, a medical doctor, had him undergo multiple evaluations by specialists to determine the underlying reason for his daily headaches.

After reviewing his history and conducting a consultation, I determined that he was a suitable candidate for neurofeedback therapy. Since he resided out of state, I informed him that I would connect him with a BrainCore colleague near his location for the qEEG brain mappings. This eliminated the need for him to travel to Duluth, Georgia for follow-up brain mappings. He was delighted to hear this!

He also shared that he was a track coach and had been a track athlete in high school. Despite his daily headaches, he managed to consistently coach his track team and train with them. I commended him for his commitment to staying active despite his chronic migraines. I also emphasized the importance of a daily dose of vitamin D for maintaining positive mental health.

I inquired about his readiness to begin my program. He expressed his desire to discuss it with his wife before making a decision. After not hearing back from him, I followed up a few days later. He informed me that he had decided against pursuing my program due to their son's upcoming college expenses. I expressed my understanding while emphasizing the importance of self-care. I highlighted the lengthy duration of his headaches, eleven years, and empathized with the challenges he faced. I shared my own experience of becoming easily irritable even with mild headaches and couldn't imagine coping with daily migraines with the same composure. He acknowledged his adaptation to the condition, stating that he had "gotten used to it."

I assured him that I would continue to check in on him every few weeks to monitor his progress. He expressed his gratitude for my concern. As time progressed, I periodically reached out to him. He informed me that their son was thriving in college. I inquired whether his headaches had shown any improvement, but he sadly replied that they persisted. More time elapsed, and I continued to call him, extending the intervals between check-ins. Eventually, I removed him from my callback list and kept him and his family in my prayers.

Unexpectedly, a voicemail message appeared on my account from a patient. It was from the patient. He conveyed his surprise at the two-year gap since our last conversation and expressed his disappointment as his condition remained unchanged over that period. The debilitating daily headaches continued to disrupt his life.

I returned his call and inquired about the reason for his unexpected contact. He expressed frustration and disbelief that two years had passed without any improvement in his condition or overall well-being. His daily routine remained unchanged, his outlook on life remained unchanged, and his headaches persisted relentlessly. He recognized the need for a change in his approach.

He revealed to his wife that despite fulfilling her wishes regarding traditional medical interventions, he was determined to explore alternative options. He expressed his hope for her support in pursuing neurofeedback therapy. I emphasized the importance of spousal/partner support, explaining that I no longer accept new BrainCore patients without it. I shared past experiences where patients committed to daily training sessions were undermined by negative and discouraging remarks from their spouses. I clarified that such an environment is detrimental to patient progress and recovery.

With the assurance of his wife's support, I was optimistic about his journey to becoming headache-free. The next step was to connect him with my nearest BrainCore colleague for his initial brain mapping. The beauty of the BrainCore system is that it allows patients from outside Georgia to see my colleagues and have their brain mappings performed. These mappings are then uploaded into my system after a medical release form is signed, similar to sending a patient for blood work.

Due to her demanding schedule as a medical doctor, my patient's wife was unable to be physically present for the virtual report review. However, the virtual format proved advantageous, allowing them to attend the meeting from separate locations. Upon reviewing the qEEG brain mapping, I determined that his case was more complex due to underlying metabolic concerns identified through pre-mapping screening questions. As a result, his brain was expected to respond two to three times slower to treatment compared to individuals without metabolic issues. I inquired about recent blood work to confirm that his metabolic issues were under control. He confirmed that his blood work was satisfactory. Given the complexity of his case, I recommended the program specifically designed for such instances.

Both my patient and his wife had no questions at the end of my report. His only question was regarding the start date and procedure. I explained the program details and shipped the equipment to him the following day. I reiterated my commitment to being available throughout his journey, just a phone call or text message away.

At the beginning of his program, my patient understandably experienced frustration. As explained, when his brain was in the correct frequency, the streaming service video would be bright and clear, and the audio would be audible. Conversely, when his brain was in the incorrect frequency, the screen would dim, and the volume would decrease. This initial lack of visual and auditory feedback understandably caused frustration. I suggested he adjust the sound level to maintain some audio and enable closed captions to follow the visual content. He appreciated the suggestions.

I reminded him that his symptoms and condition developed gradually, not overnight. Similarly, neurofeedback therapy, despite its effectiveness, does not produce immediate results for most individuals. While I understood his frustration with the temporary loss of audio and video feedback, I wanted to manage his expectations and emphasize the importance of patience in this process.

As I do with all my patients, I inquired about chiropractic care. Some may find this question unusual, and I've been asked how, as a chiropractor, I decided to incorporate neurofeedback therapy into my practice. What many people don't realize is that chiropractors focus on the nervous system. The brain and spinal cord are the main components of the nervous system, and the vertebral column (bones) of the spine surrounds and protects them. Chiropractic adjustments aim to ensure the nervous system functions optimally. This understanding of the nervous system made adding neurofeedback therapy a natural extension of my practice.

He informed me that he wasn't currently under chiropractic care but that the BrainCore practitioner I referred him to, was a licensed acupuncturist. He decided to incorporate acupuncture sessions alongside his neurofeedback therapy. I was pleased to hear this, as I believe in a holistic approach to healthcare, and acupuncture can be a valuable complement to neurofeedback.

After approximately five weeks of remotely monitoring his training sessions, I observed positive changes in the patterns left after he completed them. The next step was to send him to my BrainCore colleague for a follow-up brain mapping.

With follow-up brain mappings, the patient completes a few re-evaluation questionnaires to monitor progress between mappings. This provides an objective way to demonstrate progress. Not only do the patient, close family members, and friends notice changes, but they are also documented with data. Science is indeed fantastic!

After receiving the data from his second brain mapping, I entered it and ran it through the computer to generate a comparison report. The comparison report indicated that the patient had achieved a 41% total change toward normalization with his eyes closed. Recall that 20% or better toward normalization is the goal for the comparison reports. With his eyes open, he experienced a 37% total change toward normalization. These results were truly remarkable! He and his wife were thrilled with his progress thus far.

I inquired about the changes he had noticed since starting the program. He described experiencing two types of headaches before working with me: one behind his eyes and the other across the top of his head. He reported a significant reduction in the headache located at the top of his head. While the headache behind his eye persisted, its intensity had diminished considerably. He also shared that his sleep quality had improved, with only one instance of sleep talking during this period. Overall, he was sleeping soundly throughout the night without tossing and turning. These were remarkable improvements!

At his subsequent brain mapping, the comparison report indicated a 26% total change towards normalization with his eyes closed and a 39% total change towards normalization with his eyes open. While these percentages were slightly lower than the previous follow-up, they still demonstrated continued progress. I reminded him and his wife of the complexity of the brain, comparing it to a Rubik's Cube in the context of neurofeedback therapy. Sometimes, taking a step back is necessary to progress forward. Fortunately, they were both within my age range and readily understood this analogy.

During our next conversation, I again inquired about the changes he had noticed since the last brain mapping. He mentioned that he had increased his exercise frequency and now maintained a more regular sleep and work schedule. Additionally, he had been drinking more water. As part of my program, I offer one-on-one sessions with patients to provide them with tools and strategies for maximizing the benefits of therapy. In this patient's case, his homework included increasing his daily water intake to half his body weight in ounces and scheduling an appointment with an endocrinologist for blood work. He was also instructed to bring the results of this blood work to the functional medicine specialist at my BrainCore colleague's office. I encouraged him to continue making progress, and he expressed his commitment to doing so.

It was time for my patient's final brain mapping under my program. The comparison report revealed a remarkable 26% total change toward normalization with his eyes closed and a staggering 51% total change toward normalization with his eyes open. I eagerly inquired about his progress during this final round of therapy.

He enthusiastically shared that he was no longer plagued by nightmares and was experiencing a significant improvement in sleep quality. He expressed how the headaches had severely impacted his overall well-being, but he now felt like he was firmly in control of his life. With a heartfelt "hallelujah," he declared that he was no longer walking around like a zombie for most of the day. His body no longer dictated his wake-up time, which had previously been as late as noon despite his workday starting hours earlier.

He revealed that his journey to recovery began with a recommendation from a family friend who had heard me on a podcast years ago. This friend, who was a participant on the show, recognized the potential benefits of neurofeedback therapy for my patient and shared the information with his mother. This serendipitous connection led my patient to my practice, setting in motion the remarkable transformation of his life.

Recently, my patient reached out to me with exciting news. He had not only won the triple jump at the Nationals competition but had also been crowned the USA Track and Field national champion in the triple jump for his age group (50-54 years old). He expressed his heartfelt gratitude to both me and the acupuncturist for our unwavering support throughout his journey. With renewed determination, he set his sights on even greater achievements, aiming for the world title and the American/world age group records. He acknowledged the challenges of Master's track but expressed his appreciation for the role we had played in paving his way to success. His final words were a resounding "*THANK YOU*" in all caps.

The wonderful news continued to flow! In a recent update, he shared his latest accomplishments, stating, "*I am glad to say I won my first international competition.*" He went on to express his profound gratitude for the "life wins" he was experiencing at this stage of his life. He concluded by declaring, "*I ended my first year in Masters track and field as the #1 US triple jumper in my age group and #12 in the world. Looking forward to improving on that ranking next year. Thank you again for your part in this win. You are a true GOD SEND.*"

I am deeply touched by my patient's transformation and his remarkable achievements. His story serves as a testament to the power of neurofeedback therapy and the importance of collaboration in achieving one's goals. I am honored to have played a part in his journey and wish him continued success in his athletic endeavors.

Image 11A

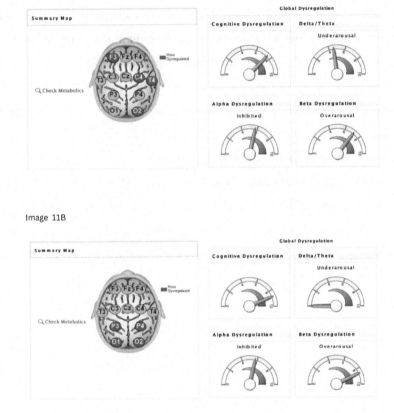

Image 11B

Helping families through neurofeedback therapy is my *joy*. I live for the transformations that I see in my patients and their loved ones. When a patient comes to me suffering from a wealth of symptoms from various mental health challenges, I am humbled by their trust. I am hopeful that those symptoms will lessen or disappear after completing one of my programs, and I am grateful when their lives have been drastically changed for the better.

Neurofeedback therapy can have a ripple effect throughout a family. When one person changes, it can inspire and empower others to change as well. As a result, everyone who interacts with that person can have a better experience.

I have seen firsthand how neurofeedback therapy can transform families. I have seen parents become more patient and understanding, children become more confident and self-assured, and siblings become more supportive and loving. I am so grateful for the opportunity to help families heal and thrive.

Testimonial by Deirdre Wheeler

Dr. Holmes is amazing, professional, caring and a great doctor! Neurofeedback Therapy has helped me tremendously. I had a very bad concussion and was struggling to heal from it. Not only has the therapy helped with that it has also helped with my insomnia, anxiety and general mood!! Thank [you] Dr. Holmes!

CHAPTER 10

Unveiling the Roots of Mental Health Challenges and Crafting Powerful Options

"Difficult roads often lead to beautiful destinations.
The best is yet to come."
Zig Ziglar

I used to hold the belief that people were born with certain predispositions that later manifested as mental health conditions and differences. Now, I recognize that a complex interplay of factors shapes brain development and mental well-being.

While genetics contribute to certain conditions and challenges, emotional, physical, sexual, verbal, and mental stressors also play a significant role. An example of an emotional trauma is the loss of a parent at a tender age, especially when witnessed violently. It's perplexing how some individuals who experienced such profound loss had relatives around them who, overwhelmed by their own shock and distress, failed to recognize or seek professional counseling for these children's grief, post-traumatic events, or other mental health needs.

These adults were grappling with their own mental health struggles and were unable to provide adequate support to their young ones. Truthfully, a significant portion of the patients I encounter in my practice bear the scars of childhood emotional trauma.

Physical traumas encompass physical abuse by a parent, relative, or caregiver. In extreme cases, children are subjected to abuse with objects like belts, shoes, wooden spoons, extension cords, fists, and more. It's crucial to distinguish between abuse and discipline. Unfortunately, when a parent is experiencing immense stress and trauma, operating in a survival mode, it becomes difficult to think rationally when additional stress arises, especially from a child. This can be the tipping point, the final straw that breaks the camel's back, leading to the childbearing the brunt of their parent's frustration. Granted, there are instances where a child's inappropriate behavior triggers parental outbursts, but these reactions stem from unresolved trauma rather than genuine discipline.

Another possible cause of mental health differences, stems from exposure to vaccines, toxins, and drugs. These substances often contain components that can be harmful to the body and the nervous system. Some toxins can even be environmental, such as air pollution, water pollution, and noise pollution.

I've always found it puzzling that as our environment becomes more sophisticated, more vaccines seem to be introduced. We've made tremendous strides in hygiene and daily practices to reduce exposure to harmful diseases, yet more vaccines exist today than when I was born 50 years ago. This doesn't quite make sense to me.

I believe we should carefully consider the potential risks and benefits before administering vaccines. I'm also a proponent of using natural remedies and supplements whenever possible to minimize the risk of adverse reactions or complications.

Medications are another area where I have reservations. While they can be lifesavers in certain situations, they're not always the answer. I'm a firm believer in listening to our bodies and using natural remedies whenever possible. It's quite possible that the medications we take have side effects that are worse than the conditions they're intended to treat.

Perceived threats can also contribute to mental health challenges. I recently learned about two additional aspects of the fight-or-flight response: freeze and fawn. Freezing is when the body shuts down, and the person may not experience any emotions at all. Fawn is a response coined by therapist Pete Walker, where a person tries to please or appease a threat to avoid further harm. I personally relate to the freeze response.

One night, as I was getting out of my parents' car after returning from a movie, my brother jumped out of the bushes. I'm not sure how long he was hiding, but he startled me. I was so scared that I couldn't move a muscle. Remember when you watch those horror movies, and the person just stands there as danger approaches? We end up yelling at the person in the movie to run! Run! Why are you standing there? Run! Yeah, that's exactly what happened to me. My body just froze up, and I couldn't move. I completely understand the freeze response now.

The freeze and fawn responses can have a significant impact on mental health. They can lead to anxious thoughts, depressed moods, and stress from post-traumatic events. If you're struggling with these challenges, it's important to seek professional help. There are effective modalities available, such as neurofeedback therapy, that can help you manage and mitigate your symptoms and improve your quality of life.

Another cause of mental health differences stems from a nervous system that isn't functioning properly due to spinal subluxations or misalignments.

The nervous system is a complex network of nerves and cells that transmit signals throughout the body. It's responsible for everything from controlling our movements to regulating our emotions. When the nervous system is functioning properly, we feel our best both physically and mentally.

However, when the nervous system is out of alignment, it can lead to a variety of problems, including pain, fatigue, and digestive issues. It can also contribute to mental health challenges, such as anxious thoughts, depressed moods, and the sleep challenges.

Spinal subluxations are misalignments of the bones in the spine. These misalignments can occur as a result of various traumas to the body, from birth throughout adulthood. When a spinal subluxation occurs, it can put pressure on the nerves in the spine, interfering with their ability to send and receive signals properly.

Chiropractors are trained to identify and correct spinal subluxations. By realigning the spine, chiropractors help to restore proper function to the nervous system. This can lead to a variety of benefits, including:

- Improved pain relief

- Increased energy levels

- Enhanced immune system function

- Reduced stress and anxiety

- Improved sleep quality

In addition to its physical benefits, chiropractic care can also have a positive impact on mental health. By improving the nervous system's function, chiropractic care can help to reduce symptoms of anxious thoughts, depressed moods, and stressful traumatic events.

If you're struggling with any of these mental health challenges, I encourage you to talk to your chiropractor. They may be able to help you feel better both physically and mentally.

It's important to remember that chiropractic care is a proactive approach to health. Instead of waiting until you're already experiencing problems, regular chiropractic adjustments can help to keep your spine in alignment and your nervous system functioning at its best.

So, if you're looking for a way to improve your overall health and well-being, I encourage you to consider chiropractic care.

In chiropractic school, I was introduced to the five Pillars of Health These pillars encompass essential aspects of a healthy lifestyle: diet, exercise, water consumption, sleep, and a positive mindset.

Diet

When people hear the word "diet," they often think of restrictive food plans that limit what they can eat. However, a true dietary approach to health is about making conscious choices about the foods and beverages you consume, focusing on nutrient-rich, whole foods that nourish your body. It's about embracing a lifestyle of eating that supports your overall well-being.

Prioritize consuming clean, unprocessed foods that are as close to their natural state as possible. This means choosing whole grains, fresh fruits and vegetables, lean proteins, and healthy fats. Limit your intake of processed foods, sugary drinks, and excessive amounts of added sugars and preservatives.

Exercise

The mere mention of the word "exercise" can make people's eyes widen and a look of apprehension cross their faces. What many fail to realize is that even a simple 30-minute walk three to four times a week can significantly impact your overall health and well-being. Walking is an excellent form of exercise, and brisk walking is even better! Studies have shown that individuals who engage in brisk walking live an average of 12 to 15 years longer than those who walk at a leisurely pace.

Benefits of Brisk Walking

Brisk walking offers a multitude of health benefits, including:

- Improved cardiovascular health: Brisk walking strengthens the heart and improves circulation, reducing the risk of heart disease, stroke, and high blood pressure.

- Enhanced weight management: Brisk walking burns calories, aiding in weight loss or maintenance.

- Strengthened bones and muscles: Brisk walking promotes bone density and muscle strength, reducing the risk of osteoporosis and fractures.

- Elevated mood: Brisk walking releases endorphins, natural mood-elevating chemicals that can combat stress, anxiety, and depression.

Water Consumption

Adequate water intake is crucial for optimal health. Water plays a vital role in various bodily functions, from regulating temperature to transporting nutrients and flushing out waste products.

While there is no one-size-fits-all recommendation for water intake, the general guideline suggests consuming half of your body weight in ounces of water daily. For instance, if you weigh 150 pounds, aim to drink around 75 ounces of water per day.

However, it's important to individualize your water needs based on factors such as your activity level, climate, and overall health. If you engage in strenuous exercise or live in a hot climate, you may need to increase your water intake accordingly.

Mindful Water Consumption

While water is essential for hydration, overconsumption can be detrimental to your health. Consuming excessive amounts of water can lead to water intoxication, a condition that can disrupt electrolyte balance and cause various symptoms, including nausea, vomiting, and muscle cramps.

Listen to your body's cues and drink water when you feel thirsty. Avoid forcing yourself to consume large quantities of water just to meet an arbitrary daily goal.

Sleeping

Just as a cellphone that hasn't been shut down for an extended period will eventually malfunction, so does our body when deprived of adequate sleep. The average adult requires around seven hours of sleep per night to function optimally. While infants and teenagers require more sleep, adults need at least seven hours to allow their brains and bodies to rest, repair, and rejuvenate.

Importance of Sleep

Sleep is essential for numerous bodily functions, including:

- Memory consolidation: Sleep plays a crucial role in converting short-term memories into long-term ones, ensuring we retain information and experiences.

- Emotional regulation: Adequate sleep helps manage emotions and reduce stress, promoting emotional well-being.

- Physical restoration: Sleep allows the body to repair and rebuild tissues, muscles, and bones.

Tips for Better Sleep

In today's technology-driven world, distractions like smartphones, televisions, and computers can disrupt sleep patterns. To promote better sleep:

- Create a consistent sleep schedule: Aim to go to bed and wake up at the same time each day, even on weekends.

- Establish a relaxing bedtime routine: Engage in calming activities like reading or taking a warm bath before bed.

- Minimize light exposure: Avoid screens and bright lights for at least an hour before bed.

- Create a comfortable sleep environment: Ensure your bedroom is dark, quiet, and cool.

Optimizing Sleep Quality: Setting the Stage for Optimal Health

Achieving adequate sleep is crucial for overall health and well-being. However, the quality of our sleep is just as important as the quantity. By creating an optimal sleep environment, we can enhance our sleep quality and reap the numerous benefits it offers.

The Ideal Sleep Temperature

Research suggests that maintaining a cool and comfortable bedroom temperature, around 65°F, can significantly improve sleep quality. This temperature promotes relaxation and helps the body transition into the deeper stages of sleep, including REM sleep, which is essential for memory consolidation, emotional processing, and overall brain health.

Benefits of Quality Sleep

The benefits of quality sleep extend far beyond feeling refreshed and energized. It plays a vital role in maintaining physical and mental health, contributing to:

- Improved Mood: Sufficient sleep helps regulate hormones that influence mood, reducing the risk of depression and anxiety.

- Reduced Stress: Sleep allows the body to recover from stress, promoting a sense of calm and balance.

- Healthy Weight Management: Sleep deprivation can disrupt hormones that regulate appetite, leading to weight gain and increased risk of obesity.

- Enhanced Productivity: Sleep deprivation impairs cognitive function, making it difficult to concentrate, learn, and perform tasks effectively.

- Boosted Immune System: Sleep plays a crucial role in immune function, helping the body fight off infections and illnesses.

- Improved Memory: Sleep is essential for memory consolidation, the process of transferring short-term memories into long-term storage.

- Strengthened Emotional Processing: Sleep allows the brain to process and integrate emotional experiences, promoting emotional resilience and well-being.

Addressing Sleep Difficulties

If you're experiencing difficulty sleeping, there are several strategies you can try to improve your sleep quality:

- Establish a Regular Sleep Schedule: Go to bed and wake up at the same time each day, even on weekends, to regulate your body's natural sleep-wake cycle.

- Create a Relaxing Bedtime Routine: An hour or two before bed, engage in calming activities such as reading, taking a warm bath, or listening to soothing music. Avoid using electronic devices, as the blue light emitted from their screens can interfere with sleep.

- Optimize Your Sleep Environment: Ensure your bedroom is dark, quiet, and cool to promote relaxation and restful sleep.

- Avoid Caffeine and Alcohol Before Bed: Caffeine and alcohol can disrupt sleep patterns and make it difficult to fall asleep or stay asleep.

- Regular Exercise: Regular physical activity can improve sleep quality, but avoid strenuous workouts close to bedtime.

- Neurofeedback Therapy: Neurofeedback therapy can help train the brain to regulate sleep patterns and improve sleep quality.

Remember, sleep is not a luxury; it's a biological necessity for optimal health and well-being. By prioritizing sleep quality and creating a conducive sleep environment, you can unlock a range of benefits that will enhance your physical and mental well-being. Be sure to download your free Bedtime Bliss Blueprint!

Maintaining a Positive Mindset: Nurturing Your Inner Voice

We've all heard the expression "garbage in, garbage out." This concept applies to our mental state as well. The thoughts we cultivate within ourselves have a profound impact on our overall well-being.

In chiropractic school, we are continuously reminded of the importance of paying close attention to our internal dialogue. Negative self-talk is a prevalent issue, and its detrimental effects on our mental health cannot be overlooked. I encourage my patients to incorporate daily walks into their routine, not only to boost their vitamin D intake, which is crucial for mental health, but also to help clear their minds of negative self-talk.

The more we reinforce negative thoughts, the more likely our brains are to enter a state of fight-or-flight, even when the perceived threat originates from within. One negative thought can snowball into a cascade of negativity, leading to self-loathing and despair.

I don't allow my patients to engage in negative self-talk in my presence. It's often surprising to them when I gently redirect their negative thought patterns. Many of them are unaware of their self-deprecating language because it has become so ingrained.

Negative thought patterns often stem from intergenerational transmission. Parents' negative self-talk can become embedded in their children's subconscious, shaping their perceptions of themselves and the world. While parents often intend to protect their children with their words, these negative messages can have a lasting impact, leading to self-doubt and insecurity.

Parents, please speak life into your children. Speak positively over them and encourage their growth. Even when they make decisions you disagree with, strive to be supportive and positive. While guiding them with your wisdom, avoid burdening them with your fears and anxieties. These negative emotions can be paralyzing, hindering your child's development and potentially leading them to become fearful and inhibited adults. Unfortunately, this cycle of negativity can perpetuate itself, passing from generation to generation.

Breaking the Cycle of Negativity

To break this cycle, it's essential to actively cultivate a positive mindset. Here are some practical strategies to get started:

- Challenge Negative Thoughts: Question the validity of negative thoughts that arise. Are they based on facts or just distorted perceptions?

- Reframe Your Thinking: Consciously reframe negative thoughts into more positive and realistic ones. For instance, instead of thinking "I'm a failure," try "I'm learning and growing."

- Practice Daily Gratitude: Regularly reflect on the things you're thankful for. This shifts your focus from negative aspects to positive ones.

- Surround Yourself with Positivity: Seek out positive influences in your life, whether it's friends, family, or supportive communities.

- Seek Professional Help: If negative thoughts are overwhelming and affecting your daily life, don't hesitate to seek professional help from a therapist or counselor.

Remember, cultivating a positive mindset takes time and consistent effort. Be patient with yourself and celebrate your progress along the way. By nurturing your inner voice with positive thoughts, you can create a more fulfilling and joyful life for yourself.

The Power of the Five Pillars of Health

By incorporating the five pillars of health – diet, exercise, water consumption, sleep, and a positive mindset – into your daily life, you can lay a solid foundation for overall well-being. These pillars work synergistically to enhance your physical and mental health, boost energy levels, and promote a greater sense of vitality. Embrace these principles and experience the transformative power of a holistic approach to health.

Taking steps to calm and maintain a healthy nervous system is crucial for overall well-being. One effective way to promote nervous system health is through regular chiropractic adjustments. Chiropractic care aims to align the spine, which in turn helps to improve nerve function and reduce stress on the nervous system.

Personally, I receive chiropractic adjustments weekly and find them to be incredibly beneficial. When I go too long without an adjustment, I notice a significant difference in my overall health and well-being. My body feels out of balance, and I experience a lack of energy and motivation.

It's essential to remember that lasting change requires consistent effort. Without making conscious and sustainable changes to your daily routine, it's difficult to achieve the desired outcomes. By incorporating regular chiropractic adjustments, along with a holistic approach to wellness, you can cultivate a calmer, more balanced nervous system, leading to enhanced mental health and overall well-being.

Navigating the Path to Mental Wellness: Exploring Neurofeedback Therapy

Mental health and well-being encompass a range of factors, including emotional, psychological, and social aspects. When facing challenges in these areas, individuals often seek out various methods and therapies to regain balance and improve their overall well-being.

A Multifaceted Approach to Mental Wellness

Numerous approaches exist to address mental health concerns. Some common methods include:

- Cognitive-Behavioral Therapy (CBT): A form of psychotherapy that focuses on identifying and changing unhelpful thought patterns and behaviors.

- Occupational Therapy (OT): A healthcare profession that helps individuals regain or maintain the skills they need to perform daily activities.

- Psychology and psychiatry: Medical specialties that focus on the diagnosis, treatment, and prevention of mental disorders.

- Eye movement desensitization and reprocessing (EMDR): A therapy that uses eye movements to address trauma and emotional distress.

- Chiropractic care: A complementary and alternative medicine practice that focuses on the spine and its connection to the nervous system.

- Speech therapy: A profession that helps individuals with communication and swallowing disorders.

- Vision therapy: A specialized form of optometry that addresses vision problems that are not correctable with glasses or contact lenses.

- Music therapy: A therapeutic use of music to improve physical, emotional, and mental health.

- Ketamine therapy: A rapidly growing treatment for depression and other mental health conditions.

- Counseling: A general term for providing professional guidance and support to individuals facing personal or emotional challenges.

- Applied Behavioral Analysis (ABA): A therapy that focuses on applying principles of behaviorism to change behavior.

- Hyperbaric chambers: Devices that deliver increased atmospheric pressure to promote healing and oxygenation of tissues.

- Executive function coaching: A type of coaching that helps individuals develop and strengthen their executive functions, such as planning, organizing, and self-control.

- ADHD counseling: Specialized counseling for individuals with attention deficit hyperactivity disorder (ADHD).

- Tapping: A technique that involves stimulating specific points on the body to release emotional and physical tension.

- Supplements: Nutritional supplements that may offer mental health benefits, such as omega-3 fatty acids and vitamin D.

- Meditation: A practice that focuses on training the mind to achieve a state of calmness and clarity.

- Dialectical Behavior Therapy (DBT): A type of therapy that teaches individuals skills to manage emotions, tolerate distress, and improve relationships.

- Medications: Pharmaceutical drugs prescribed to treat mental health conditions, such as antidepressants and anti-anxiety medications.

- Nutritional changes: Dietary modifications that may support mental health, such as reducing processed foods and increasing intake of fruits and vegetables.

- Drinking alkaline water: Consuming water with a higher pH level, which some proponents believe may have health benefits.

- Imagery counseling: A therapy that uses guided imagery to promote relaxation, address fears, and enhance self-awareness.

- Prayer: A spiritual practice that involves connecting with a higher power or seeking divine guidance.

- Melatonin: A hormone that regulates sleep and may also have mood-regulating effects.

- CBD or cannabis products: Cannabidiol (CBD) is a non-psychoactive compound found in cannabis that is being studied for its potential therapeutic benefits, including reducing anxiety and improving sleep.

- Life coaching: A form of personal development that helps individuals set goals, identify obstacles, and develop strategies for achieving their goals.

The Uniqueness of Neurofeedback Therapy

Neurofeedback therapy stands out among these various approaches as a non-invasive, drug-free method that directly targets brain activity. It involves training individuals to self-regulate their brain waves, potentially leading to improvements in a range of mental health conditions.

While neurofeedback may not be suitable for everyone, it has demonstrated promising results in addressing various mental health concerns, including:

- Anxious thoughts

- Depressed moods

- Attention and focus challenges

- Stress from traumatic events

- Autism spectrum disorder (ASD)

- Epilepsy

- Sleep disorders

Choosing the Right Path for You

With the vast array of options available, selecting the most appropriate treatment approach can be a daunting task. It's crucial to consider individual factors such as the specific mental health concerns, personal preferences, and compatibility with existing treatment plans.

Neurofeedback therapy offers a unique and potentially effective approach to mental wellness. If you're considering neurofeedback, it's important to consult with a qualified practitioner who can assess your suitability and guide you through the process.

Remember, embarking on a journey of mental health improvement requires patience, dedication, and an open mind. Explore the various options available, seek professional guidance, and find the path that best aligns with your individual needs.

Neurofeedback Therapy: Transforming Lives Through the Renewal of Minds

Not everyone is a candidate for neurofeedback therapy. Some conditions, such as late-stage dementia and Parkinson's, may only benefit from symptom mitigation. My office requires a commitment to the program, and I value partnering with those who are ready to transform their lives through the renewal of their minds (Romans 12:2 NIV).

Our Vision

Our vision is to raise global awareness and create opportunities for this natural drug-free therapy that addresses mental health and wellness challenges.

Our Values

Our values are love, service, health, quality of life, and independence.

- We show love to our clients, so they know they are supported, respected, heard, and valued.

- We care for others with joy, fulfillment, and individual vitality.

- We propel our clients to enhance their mental, spiritual, and individual well-being.

- We enrich their lives so they can experience life with more ease.

- We provide the opportunity to attain independence and self-sufficiency so they can truly thrive.

How to Get Started

Here's how to start the process of being transformed by the renewing of your mind through neurofeedback therapy:

1. Contact us for a discovery call. We will let you know if neurofeedback therapy is a good fit for you or a loved one.

2. Schedule your consultation.

3. Begin your journey to mental wellness.

Please note:. Our programs are open to individuals residing in the contiguous United States. You don't have to live in Georgia to embark on your mental health and wellness journey with us.

Contact Information

- https://bookwithdrh.com

- 470-535-0506

I look forward to helping you achieve your mental health and wellness goals.

In addition to the above, I would also like to add the following:

- Neurofeedback therapy is a safe and effective modality for a variety of mental health conditions as well as for optimal brain performance.

- Neurofeedback therapy can be used to improve sleep quality, attention, and focus.

- Neurofeedback therapy can help people to better manage stress and cope with difficult emotions.

- Neurofeedback therapy is a drug-free and non-invasive method, making it a safe and desirable option for many people.

Now that you've taken this important step in considering neurofeedback therapy, know that I am here to support you further. Whether you have questions or are ready to schedule a discovery call, I am committed to helping you discern if neurofeedback therapy is the right path for your wellness goals. Let's work together to unlock your full potential for mental wellness.

Author Bio

D r. Candace Holmes, BrainCore certified Neurofeedback Therapy Practitioner and chiropractor, combines eight years of neurofeedback therapy expertise with twenty-five years in chiropractic care. Witnessing her daughter's remarkable ADHD transformation led her to integrate neurofeedback into her practice. Dr. Holmes shares her insights at events like the American Business Women's Association, ProWin, and the Duluth Rotary Club. Recognized as Alignable's Local Business Person of the Year in Duluth, Georgia, she resides in metro Atlanta with her two daughters. Outside of work, she enjoys nature walks, travel, reading, fine dining, and roller skating.

URGENT PLEA!

Thank You For Reading My Book!
I really appreciate all of your feedback and
I love hearing what you have to say.

Please take two minutes now to leave a helpful review on
Amazon letting me know what you thought of the book:
braincoreofduluth.com/bookreview
Thanks so much!
-Dr. Holmes